QUEUE TIPS

Discovering Your Next Great Movie

ROB CHRISTOPHER

GUEST STARRING

Julia Sweeney
Barry Gifford
Ken Vandermark
Halley Feiffer
Jeff "Beachbum" Berry
Zoe Trope
Bilge Ebiri
Bill Ott
David Kodeski
Eugenia Williamson

an imprint of the American Library Association

HURON STREET | PRESS

CHICAGO · 2013

ROB CHRISTOPHER has covered film, cocktails, and sundry other Chicago topics for the website Chicagoist since 2006. Author of the book *100 Spinning Plates,* he has also written articles for such publications as the *Chicago Reader* and *American Libraries.* He coedited the documentary *Kosher Messiah* and served as a features/documentaries programmer for the 29th Reeling Film Festival. He wrote the introduction to the young adult edition of *Sad Stories of the Death of Kings,* by Barry Gifford. An active contributor to CINE-FILE, an independent cineaste web resource, he is currently working on a project titled *3 Things about 500 Movies.* He lives in Chicago. His website is randomcha.net.

Extensive effort has gone into ensuring the reliability of the information in this book; however, the publisher makes no warranty, express or implied, with respect to the material contained herein.

ISBNs: 978-1-937589-09-7 (paper); 978-1-937589-24-0 (PDF); 978-1-937589-26-4 (ePub); 978-1-937589-25-7 (Kindle).

Library of Congress Cataloging-in-Publication Data
Christopher, Robert.
    Queue tips : discovering your next great movie / by Robert Christopher.
        p. cm.
    Includes bibliographical references and index.
    ISBN 978-1-937589-09-7 (alk. paper)
    1. Motion pictures—Catalogs. 2. Motion pictures—Evaluation—Catalogs.
I. Christopher, Robert. II. Title.
    PN1998.C4535 2013
    016.79143—dc23   2012023938

Cover design by Adrianna Sutton. Image © Shutterstock, Inc.
Text design by Karen Sheets de Gracia in Classic Round and Interstate.

♾ This paper meets the requirements of ANSI/NISO Z39.48–1992 (Permanence of Paper).
Printed in the United States of America
17 16 15 14 13   5 4 3 2 1

For Andy,

who has watched more wonderful and more terrible
and just more movies period with me than anyone else

Contents

Acknowledgments

My thanks and appreciation to everyone who supported me throughout the writing of this book, as well as those who have helped me observe movies more closely, including B. Frayn Masters, Dan Kraus, Dylan Lorenz, Jessi Hill, Jill Davis, J. Michael Jeffers, Kevin Sampsell, Mary Mackay, Scott Smith, Steven Pate, Tchavdar Georgiev, and my fellow contributors at CINE-FILE. Thanks, Mom and Dad. And a special thank-you to Margaret Lyons, who unknowingly coined the book's title during a casual conversation in 2008.

Introduction

AT THE HEART OF CINEMA IS A LIBRARY

Because this book is published by the American Library Association, you may be wondering what movies have to do with libraries.

Flash back to the early 1990s, when the DVD was only a twinkle in Toshiba's eye and streaming video was science fiction. My freshman year of college in Chicago, I lived in a dorm downtown in the Loop. The Harold Washington Library, the main library of the Chicago Public Library system, was only a few blocks away. Sure, I went there to do research on my classwork. But as a budding, obsessive cinephile, the best thing about the Harold Washington was the gigantic VHS collection. I could check out three movies for the weekend, take them back to my dorm room, and have my own triple feature. Which I did. A lot.

I often think back to a particular weekend when I checked out *Doctor Zhivago*. For its visual splendor alone, magnificently photographed in an ultra widescreen process called Panavision 70, it's certainly one of the greatest epics ever made. It was designed to be projected onto a giant screen, sporting a multichannel stereo soundtrack meant to impress. It's a movie that typifies what it means to Go To The Movies. As awesome as one's home setup might be, I still maintain that there's no experience comparable to seeing a movie on the big screen, in a theater. While the movie unspools in a darkened theater, you're locked in its spell. If it's doing its job, you forget about the outside world and give yourself over to its dream world. Sitting on the couch at home, there are too many tempting distractions: your computer, your cell phone, that bag of chips calling to you from the pantry, your significant other pestering you about taking out the trash.

But back to that college weekend. I had never seen *Doctor Zhivago* before. It was so long it spread across two tapes. I watched it on the 13-inch TV/VCR combo I had in my dorm room, and the VHS version I checked out from the library was a pan-and-scan transfer that chopped off a great deal of the picture. Furthermore, my little TV boasted only a tiny built-in speaker; Maurice Jarre's lush, haunting "Lara's Theme" was little more than a catchy melody.

Despite my watching it on a 13-inch screen with crummy sound, *Doctor Zhivago* still blew me away. It wasn't until years later that I was able to see it the way it was designed to be seen, in a proper theater, complete with wide screen and surround sound. An experience that was infinitely superior. Yet I might not have seen it or many other great movies in the first place were it not for the Harold Washington Library and its excellent selection of videos. The closest video store to my dorm was almost a mile away; besides, renting movies was expensive (for the poor college student that I was, at any rate), but I could check out tapes from the library for a dollar each. At that price I could watch all the movies I'd read about in my movie books, and I could also check out random stuff that just looked interesting. (*Umberto D,* included in this book, was just such a movie.)

For a dollar, you're willing to take a chance. It's the whole model that Redbox is built on. Set up near the entrances of grocery stores, drugstores, and convenience stores, Redbox kiosks function like self-contained quick-fix dollar stores for videos. The crucial difference between a library collection and Redbox is that the average Redbox kiosk gives you the choice of a few dozen movies—only the most popular rentals, meaning that practically all of them are less than two years old. If you're looking for a documentary, or something that's not in English, or (gasp!) a black-and-white movie, you're pretty much out of luck.

A library like Harold Washington has hundreds of movies, spanning genre, subject, and language. Libraries are also staffed by dedicated individuals who are trained to help you find what you're looking for, even if you're not quite sure what you're looking for. Those things haven't changed since I was in college, but a lot of other things have. Sadly, the independent local video store, proudly owned and operated by movie nerds and stocked with a deep catalog of titles, has become an endangered species. First it was squeezed by the dominance of huge chains like Blockbuster, and now it's under attack by the likes of Netflix and online video, not to mention piracy. That makes libraries, with their knowledgeable staff and wide selection of DVDs, more important than ever. If you've never thought to take a look at your local library, or talk movies with your friendly neighborhood librarian, here's hoping that *Queue Tips* will be the catalyst.

But the value of libraries reaches far beyond the materials they circulate. When it comes to the history of cinema, great libraries and archives around the world have helped preserve thousands of films that otherwise would have been lost forever. Martin Scorsese's Film Foundation estimates that 90 percent of all American silent films and 50 percent of American sound films made before 1950 no longer exist. At all. In any form. Period. Many of these films were lost because of poor storage conditions or fire; but many were just thrown out, trashed by companies who concluded that they had no commercial value and simply weren't worth keeping.

Initiatives like the National Film Registry at the Library of Congress, which I detail in chapter 3, are important advocates for film preservation. However, it's crucial to note that just because a movie is on the National Film Registry doesn't mean that it's actually safe—it only means that it's been deemed worthy of saving. And these aren't just musty old movies we're talking about. When Francis Ford Coppola undertook a restoration of *The Godfather* a few years ago, film-preservation expert Robert A. Harris was shocked to discover that the original negative was riddled with scratches and dirt and severely torn in several places. The restoration, bankrolled by Paramount, ultimately cost millions of dollars. But for every blockbuster like *The Godfather* that has a deep-pocketed studio benefactor ready to save the day, there are hundreds of neglected and semiforgotten movies languishing on shelves. Fortunately many archives and libraries are undertaking preservation efforts. The UCLA Film and Television Archive, the Academy of Motion Picture Arts and Sciences, Anthology Film Archives, George Eastman House, and hundreds of other institutions all over the world are doing the crucial work of rescuing and restoring vulnerable films.

Another challenge is making these films available to audiences. When, in an infamous letter to subscribers, Netflix CEO Reed Hastings wrote that "nearly every movie ever made is published on DVD," he was dead wrong. The fact is that there are literally thousands, if not tens of thousands, of movies that have yet to be made available on video. That's why local and repertory movie houses are the true heroes of film exhibition. The tireless work of their programmers and bookers in tracking down rare prints of films—some of which still linger in obscurity and have never been released on video—keeps movie history alive by putting all kinds of movies exactly where they belong: in front of audiences. And the passion of these cinephiles often triggers the appearance of these would-be lost films on home video. There's a certain degree of irony here. With many movie houses now entirely switched over to digital projection, and with flat-screen TVs and home theater systems quickly becoming the living-room norm, the technical difference between watching a movie in public or at home is narrowing.

In the grand scheme of things, as my *Doctor Zhivago* story illustrates, I believe that how you go about seeing a movie is simply less important than what movie you're seeing. The technology behind it will never stop changing, but the movie's the thing. *Queue Tips* is my own modest attempt to help you discover your next great movie.

HOW TO QUEUE

It's Friday night, the end of a long week, and you'd like nothing better than to watch a great movie and be transported somewhere else for a few hours—to be entertained and, hopefully, watch something you haven't seen a hundred times before. So what will you choose? With more movies available to watch than ever before, it's not such an easy question. In some ways having too many choices can be worse than having too few.

Why do we end up watching movies that give us so little pleasure, so much of the time? A combination of reasons. We gravitate to the familiar, even when it's mediocre, precisely because it's familiar. It's easier to settle for the known than to try something new, especially when it's movie night and whatever movie you choose has to garner the approval of everyone in your group.

Movie night can be a recurring battle, a test of wills. Namely, if we all can't agree on something, will we watch what he wants to watch or what she wants to watch or what *I* want to watch? For several years I was part of a group of friends who would get together every few weeks at someone's house to hang out, order a pizza, and watch a movie. And we faced this exact problem. Our solution was simple and, I daresay, ingenious. A week or so before movie night we would settle on a loosely defined theme ("Movies So Bad They're Good," found in this book, was one of them); since I was the organizer, everyone would e-mail me their selection. I put the title of each movie on a slip of paper. Just prior to meeting up I randomly selected one and then went to the video store and rented it. Thus, since none of us knew beforehand what that night's movie would be, none of us could bail out by using the excuses "That movie's lame" or "I've already seen that a million times." The air of mystery and anticipation about what we'd be watching always made the evening more exciting. Furthermore, since everyone got to choose a movie, it was equitable—even if we didn't watch my movie this week, I knew that sooner or later we would. Why not try something similar? Alternate who gets to choose and you'll probably discover movies you would never have watched on your own, as well as keeping everyone happy. Variety is the spice of life.

When it comes down to it, I think the biggest reason we watch so much garbage is simply that we don't think ahead. More times than not we just show up at the video store, or go online, and more or less blindly choose something. I'm not knocking spontaneity, but imagine going to a restaurant where there are hundreds of dishes on the menu. You know for a fact that the vast majority of these dishes are bland and uninspiring, but you also know that there are several that are fantastically delicious. If you don't do a little research before dinnertime—say, asking others who have eaten there or going online to find out what the food critics are saying—how do you possibly stand a chance of enjoying a tasty meal? Without a little planning, it's just a shot in the dark. I'm not suggesting that you're going to love every movie in this book, but I do hope that by reading it you'll be inspired to try some new fare instead of merely settling for the easy but bland.

"Round up the usual suspects," says Claude Rains in *Casablanca*. Well, plenty of other movie books have already done that quite well. In *Queue Tips* I've tried to round up some unusual suspects.

A queue is a line—perhaps a line you're waiting in to see a movie, or list of movies waiting to be watched. Each list in this book is just that: a list. Not *the* list. You will not find, for example, "The 10 Greatest Disaster Movies Ever Made" or "The Top 15 Movies for Kids." I'm not interested in ranking movies. What does interest me is sharing some movies you may not have heard of, and reminding you of movies you might have forgotten. I've arranged the movies in quirky lists, hoping to trigger a different way of looking at movies in general. Netflix organizes movies into rigid genre categorizations and then makes suggestions based on mysterious algorithms. These suggestions are usually far off the mark—no, if you like *The Wizard of Oz* you will probably not like the godawful Rex Harrison *Doctor Doolittle*. That kind of inflexible sorting is not very helpful; and it's certainly not fair to great filmmakers like Alfred Hitchcock, Terry Gilliam, David Lynch, and Robert Altman, whose work makes a point of straddling genre and theme. It also belittles those movies we've inadequately tagged *documentaries,* a type of work that stubbornly resists pigeonholing. A great documentary is often more gripping, moving, and insightful than a so-called fictional movie, so I see no reason to place them under quarantine in this book.

I've been fortunate enough to rope in some contributors to assist me. Film critic Bilge Ebiri shares some movies that made him love America, librarian Zoe Trope offers seven reasons to love Nicolas Cage, *Wild at Heart* author Barry Gifford chooses several flicks ideal for late-night viewing, and *Saturday Night Live* alum Julia Sweeney lists some movies that stick in her mind. Elsewhere, jazz giant Ken Vandermark examines some notable soundtracks, tiki mixologist extraordinaire Jeff "Beachbum" Berry spotlights tropical cocktails in movies, monologist David Kodeski finds homoerotic subtext in some surprising places, *Boston Phoenix* columnist Eugenia Williamson reels off some doomed movie romances, and actress Halley Feiffer (daughter of cartoonist and playwright Jules Feiffer) looks at some great film adaptations of plays. Then there's *Booklist*'s Bill Ott, who singles out ten movies that are "better than the book."

I hope this book spurs you to make some lists of your own. You could use these selections as jumping-off points for exploring a particular genre in greater depth, for example. How about an amble through the oeuvre of a favorite actor or filmmaker? Or keeping track of movies you missed at the theater so you can catch them at home? I once created a list of movies that had been remade in order to watch the original versions. You get the idea. The possibilities are endless. A little prep time goes a long way toward preventing the mindless consumption of whatever's in the New Release section.

So where do you find these movies? How do you see them? Let me return to the subject of libraries for a moment and bring up an argument that seems to crop up all the time:

"We don't need libraries anymore. Everything is online now."

News flash: it's completely untrue. And it's doubly untrue in regard to movies. Anyone who's come across a movie on Netflix or Hulu only to find the dreaded notation *currently unavailable* knows this all too well. Due to the complicated legal issues involved, finding the exact movie you want to watch via online video streaming is a crapshoot. Much like the "time holes" in *Time Bandits* (see chapter 17, "Great Movies for Tweens, Teens, and Other Kids under the Age of 99"), the various rights holders have to be in complete alignment; and since movie rights frequently expire or change hands, the window of opportunity can be short indeed.

Some might disagree, but in my opinion, physical formats like DVDs and Blu-ray discs remain the best way, at least for now, to see a movie outside of a theater. And a library can be a great place to find them. Now, I'm not suggesting that they'll have everything you'll ever want. But even if your local branch doesn't have what you're looking for, ask your librarian if it's possible to order the item from another library in the system. You might be surprised at how easy interlibrary loan can be.

Services like Netflix are obviously a great way to watch a lot of movies. You can plug many of the movies from this book directly into your queue. And Netflix is hardly the only game in town. Such companies as Blockbuster, GreenCine, and Facets also do DVD rentals by mail; and the emergence of viable video streaming, made possible by ever-faster Internet connections, has created even more avenues for watching movies. But as I've pointed out, video streaming isn't the magic solution some have claimed. Aside from the rights issues, the technology itself still has a long way to go. Because of the technical limitations—as well as the reluctance of many providers to provide high-speed Internet access to every community—watching a movie online can quickly turn into either a study in low-res pixilation or an all-you-can-eat buffet of "buffering." And where are all the wonderful special features like alternate and deleted scenes, "making of" documentaries, and filmmaker commentary tracks that you can find on the disc versions?

Nevertheless, there's something really cool about being able to surf over to Mubi and watch Luis Buñuel's *Un Chien Andalou,* a classic short that for many years was rarely shown outside of film studies classes (or the occasional David Bowie concert). Video label Criterion has partnered with Hulu to stream many titles in its catalog, and newer boutique imprints like Warner Archives, TCM Vault Collection, and MGM Limited Edition Collection (to name just a few) also stream their offerings. Amazon, Movies on Google Play, CinemaNow, Fandor, and Apple's iTunes offer thousands of movies to either stream or download. And then there are devices such as Roku and Xbox 360 that stream video directly to your TV . . .

The technology continues to improve, and thus the options for watching movies at home change so frequently that I'd be foolish to offer any kind of definitive list. But the Movie Resources section on page 131 lists some additional resources that are helpful for tracking down movies or learning more about them. In this book, we've tried to stick to movies that you have a decent chance of finding either on DVD or on streaming video. And in this age of Hollywood homogeneity, shaking up your viewing habits by supporting movies that have flown under the radar is vitally important. Check out this list of the ten highest-grossing movies of 2011 as compiled by Box Office Mojo:

1. *Harry Potter and the Deathly Hallows, Part 2*
2. *Transformers: Dark of the Moon*
3. *The Twilight Saga: Breaking Dawn, Part 1*
4. *The Hangover, Part II*
5. *Pirates of the Caribbean: On Stranger Tides*
6. *Fast Five*
7. *Mission: Impossible—Ghost Protocol*
8. *Cars 2*
9. *Sherlock Holmes: A Game of Shadows*
10. *Thor*

Notice a theme? That's nine (nine!) sequels . . . and one movie based on a comic book. No original screenplays. No documentaries. Nothing that isn't in English. Not a single film that originated outside of the Hollywood industrial complex.

The good news is that you don't have to watch that stuff. At least, not all the time. As Jonathan Rosenbaum argues (see the Movie Resources section for more about his books), there's never been a better time to be a cinephile. The world of movies is healthier than ever—outside of the Hollywood system, that is. And in the same way that you wouldn't eat at Old Country Buffet for breakfast, lunch, and dinner every day, your movie choices shouldn't be limited to whatever's showing at the multiplex in the mall, or what Redbox deigns worth stocking. Thanks to streaming video and the rise of made-on-demand services like Warner Archives; thanks to the dedication of your local film society and repertory movie theater; and especially thanks to DVDs from your library and your tenacious neighborhood video store, you have access to numberless treasures from the entire breadth of cinema.

So let's dive in, shall we?

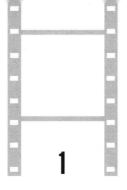

1

Ten Movies about Movies

Almost from their very beginnings, the movies have been self-reflexive, calling viewers' attention to the fact that what they're watching "is only a movie." Movies also frequently use the medium itself as a mirror. When done badly, it can be narcissistic and boring; when done successfully, it can be (to paraphrase David Byrne) a trick that also shows you how the trick is done. In the same way that the following movies use themselves to illuminate the medium, I hope this book can help you see the world of movies in new ways.

1. The Connection

1962, directed by Shirley Clarke. With Warren Finnerty, William Redfield, Carl Lee, Garry Goodrow, Jerome Raphel, Barbara Winchester, Henry Proach, Roscoe Lee Browne

Jean-Luc Godard is famously quoted as saying that "film is truth 24 times a second." But actually the full quote is "Film is truth 24 times a second, and every cut is a lie." In other words, movies can obscure as much as they reveal, which is what *The Connection* is all about. Several junkies wait in a dingy New York loft apartment for their dealer to arrive with their fix. With them is a small crew of documentary filmmakers, who have agreed to pay for their fix in exchange for filming them. The filmmakers pompously declaim that their film will show nothing but "the real

Slavoj Žižek steps into a scene from Alfred Hitchcock's *The Birds* to make a point, one of many clever moments in *The Pervert's Guide to Cinema*.

truth," but the junkies view the whole enterprise with open contempt. Locked inside a room with these characters, the movie is a study in claustrophobia. Tiny shifts in mood and behavior become changes writ large. By story's end we've studied every curl of peeling paint and black scrape on the wall; we've "lived" in that loft for two hours. That includes hanging out with legendary Blue Note jazz musicians like Freddie Redd and Jackie McLean, who provide an on-screen soundtrack. Their argot may be dated ("This cat is corroded!"), but the opportunity to watch them jam is priceless.

2. The Celluloid Closet

1996, directed by Rob Epstein and Jeffrey Friedman

Another thing about the movies—they leave plenty of room for subtext. Based on Vito Russo's book, this documentary reads between the lines of movie history, examining how the movies have portrayed gay, lesbian, bisexual, and transgendered characters from the silent age through the mid-1990s. Film clips and interviews with such figures as Tom Hanks, Tony Curtis, Whoopi Goldberg, and Gore Vidal help unearth some fascinating surprises, especially from the era when a character's sexuality could only be implied and not explicitly addressed. Two favorite clips: a fragment of silent footage shot by Thomas Edison's studio showing two men dancing together tenderly, and Vidal explaining the gay subtext of *Ben-Hur*. For more movies with sly homoeroticism, see chapter 12, "That Magic Moment: Homoerotic Display in Heteronormative Cinema."

3. The Pervert's Guide to Cinema

2006, directed by Sophie Fiennes

Speaking of subtext, here's a fascinating cine-essay that looks at the cultural baggage embedded in some well-known movies. Slovenian philosopher and cultural theorist Slavoj Žižek takes a playful journey through movies as varied as *Blue Velvet* and *Eyes Wide Shut* to *The Wizard of Oz* and *Rear Window*. And I do mean journey: Žižek is inserted in various movie locales, such as Tippi Hedren's boat in *The Birds,* while he spins analysis that's equal parts hilarious and thought-provoking. He even deconstructs the Marx Brothers (Groucho = superego; Chico = ego; Harpo = id).

4. Double Take

2009, directed by Johan Grimonprez

"If you ever meet your double, you should kill him." This ingenious, very postmodern film essay riffs on a story by novelist Tom McCarthy, imagining a 1962 meeting between Alfred Hitchcock and his doppelgänger at the Universal Studio commissary. Over this framework Grimonprez layers interviews with Hitchcock impersonator Ron Burrage, footage of the real Hitchcock, news reports from the Cold War era, and hilarious TV commercials for Folgers Coffee. This unique examination of American paranoia and showmanship is a must-see for any Hitchcock buff.

5. Henri Langlois: The Phantom of the Cinémathèque

2004, directed by Jacques Richard

At one point in this valuable documentary, Langlois, cofounder of the Cinémathèque Française, gives a tour of the objects in that institution's archive. He suddenly holds up Mother's skull from *Psycho,* casually explaining that Hitchcock wanted to give something to the Cinémathèque. Langlois was a pioneer of film preservation; during World War II he hid hundreds of films slated for destruction by the Nazis, and the Cinémathèque's collection would later grow to encompass more than sixty thousand titles. In 1974 he was awarded an honorary Oscar for his work, and this movie is an engaging portrait of an eccentric cinephile who deserves wider recognition.

6. Z Channel: A Magnificent Obsession

2004, directed by Xan Cassavetes

The work of Henri Langlois was focused on actual film prints, but since the ascendancy of TV, people have watched movies even more frequently on the tube. Launched in 1974, the Los Angeles-based Z Channel was one of the first pay cable stations in the United States. During the movie channel's fifteen-year history it broadcast a heady melange of classics, cult movies, documentaries, foreign films, "artistic" soft core, and anything else its programming director Jerry Harvey thought was worthy. He helped introduce the letterbox presentation of movies and also pioneered the notion of a director's cut by showing alternate versions of movies such as *Heaven's Gate* and *Once upon a Time in America*. Robert Altman, Quentin Tarantino, Jim Jarmusch, and others from the world of film are on hand to talk about how personally inspiring the channel was.

7. My Voyage to Italy

1999, directed by Martin Scorsese

Could there possibly be a better tour guide to the history of classic Italian cinema than Martin Scorsese? Both an ideal primer for the budding cinephile and an invigorating refresher for the seasoned film buff, Scorsese's essay unspools with contagious enthusiasm—you'll be loading up your queue in no time. His examination of the films Roberto Rossellini made with his wife Ingrid Bergman is a highlight.

8. The Player

1992, directed by Robert Altman. With Tim Robbins, Greta Scacchi, Fred Ward, Whoopi Goldberg, Peter Gallagher, Brion James, Cynthia Stevenson, Vincent D'Onofrio, Lyle Lovett

In this peerless Hollywood satire, Tim Robbins plays Griffin Mill, a paranoid film studio executive who takes matters into his own hands after receiving a series of death threats from a disgruntled screenwriter. Altman is at the top of his game right from the opening scene: an audacious seven-minute tracking shot that weaves around the studio's offices capturing various movie pitches ("It's *Out of Africa* meets *Pretty Woman*"; "It's *The Graduate* . . . *Part 2*"). A gallery of more than sixty stars play themselves.

> "I was just thinking what an interesting concept it is to eliminate the writer from the artistic process. If we could just get rid of these actors and directors, maybe we've got something here."
>
> —GRIFFIN MILL, *THE PLAYER*

9. Irma Vep

1996, directed by Olivier Assayas. With Maggie Cheung, Jean-Pierre Léaud, Nathalie Richard, Antoine Basler, Nathalie Boutefeu, Alex Descas, Dominique Faysse, Arsinée Khanjian

Hong Kong action star Maggie Cheung has been cast in the title role of Irma Vep, a slinky phantom of the night clad in a skin-tight latex Catwoman-like outfit. But when she arrives on the set she finds the production in disarray, with a director whose erratic behavior is only aggravated by his growing infatuation with her. Essentially playing a version of herself, Cheung is great fun to watch as she attempts to navigate the confusing world of international filmmaking; and as the director, French legend Jean-Pierre Léaud offers a knowing portrait of a filmmaker whose lack of inspiration has triggered a personal crisis.

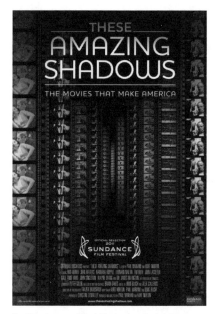

10. These Amazing Shadows

2011, directed by Paul Mariano and Kurt Norton

This documentary tells the history of the National Film Registry, featuring a number of passionate testimonials, including Christopher Nolan on *2001: A Space Odyssey*, Rob Reiner on *It's a Wonderful Life*, and John Lasseter of Pixar on the Bugs Bunny short *What's Opera, Doc?* Making a powerful case for the importance of

Paul Mariano and Kurt Norton's entertaining documentary *These Amazing Shadows* surveys some of the hundreds of classic movies listed on the National Film Registry.

film preservation, this documentary is enjoyable for even the most casual moviegoer. It's certainly a great font of suggestions for your next movie night. See chapter 3 for a list of treasures from the Registry.

2

Better Than the Book!

By Bill Ott

Bill Ott is editor and publisher of *Booklist* magazine, which has been in publication for over one hundred years and delivers more than eight thousand recommended-only reviews of books, audiobooks, reference sources, and video and DVD titles each year. Ott produces reviews for the publication as well, often in his favorite genre of crime fiction. A selection of his reviews, essays, and quizzes from *Booklist* were compiled and published as *The Back Page* (ALA, 2009).

In our secularized society, there are very few pieties left—except reading. That's why, for many, it almost borders on blasphemy to suggest that any movie could be better than the book on which it was based. Think how many postmovie discussions begin with someone saying, "Well, it wasn't nearly as good as the book." Confronted with that statement, most of us, timid souls that we are, will simply nod slowly and seriously, mumbling a quiet "of course" before going on to talk about the movie itself.

And, yet, there are times when filmmakers one-up authors, when the demands of reducing a several-hundred-page novel into a two-hour movie function not as an insurmountable barrier but as a liberating force. How often have you heard someone exclaim that this or that book needed a better editor? Sometimes the filmmaker is that editor, excising overwrought prose and stripping a story down to its essentials. It's easy to criticize a movie for mislaying the tone of a book or running roughshod over the author's voice, but there are occasions when an author's voice could use the mute button, or when an author can't keep his or her thumb off the moral scales. Trust the tale, not the teller, as D. H. Lawrence advised—and when a movie works better than its book, it's usually because the filmmakers have managed to do just that.

This list of movies better than their books ignores bad books made into less-bad films. It may well be true that the movie version of *Valley of the Dolls* was better than Jacqueline Susann's novel, but is that really a meaningful distinction? [*Rob's note:* For the answer to this question, see chapter 24, "Ten Movies So Bad They're Good."] Are Twinkies better than Ho Hos? In the ten examples listed below, both book and movie were successful critically, commercially, or both, but the movie simply did it better.

1. To Have and Have Not

1945, directed by Howard Hawks. With Humphrey Bogart, Walter Brennan, Lauren Bacall, Dolores Moran, Hoagy Carmichael, Sheldon Leonard

From the novel (1937) by Ernest Hemingway

How did Hemingway's worst novel (well, *Across the River and into the Trees* was a stinker, too) become a terrific movie, arguably the best adaption ever done from one of his books? It started with Howard Hawks, who thought the book was a "piece of junk" and felt no compunction to stick close to the story, wisely replacing Hemingway's heavy-handed Marxist polemic (the product of his involvement with the republican cause during the Spanish Civil War) with comedy and romance, which melded perfectly with the *Casablanca*-like main plot (the setting was changed from Key West to Martinique to make room for some Nazis). Kudos also go to the writers—Jules Furthman, William Faulkner, and sundry others—who turned Hemingway's sermonizing into light, witty banter (I'm betting that was due more to Furthman than to Faulkner). And let's not forget the *chemistry*—yes, chemistry—between Humphrey Bogart and 19-year-old Lauren Bacall, in her screen debut: "You know how to whistle, don't you Steve? You just put your lips together and . . . blow."

2. Out of the Past

1947, directed by Jacques Tourneur. With Robert Mitchum, Jane Greer, Kirk Douglas, Rhonda Fleming, Richard Webb, Steve Brodie

From the novel Build My Gallows High *(1946) by Geoffrey Homes*

Homes (a pseudonym for Daniel Mainwaring) wrote a perfectly satisfactory pulp thriller in 1946, but one year later, under Jacques Tourneur's direction, it became

Bogie and Bacall burn up the screen in *To Have and Have Not*. Their chemistry wasn't just good acting; they later married in real life.

what remains the greatest film noir of them all. The success of *Out of the Past* launched a long and successful screenwriting career for Mainwaring, which is a bit ironic since it's not the words that make the movie so good. Like all film noir, it's a matter of mood, and Tourneur nails it: the backlighting, the Venetian blinds, the burning cigarettes—they would all become clichés eventually, but here they are ripe with atmosphere and metaphor. And let's not forget Robert Mitchum, the greatest noir actor ever, in the role of his career. Mitchum's biographer, Lee Server, describes the essence of the actor's persona as being "his gliding, pantherlike movements, his underplaying and powerful silences, his expressive quiescence." Those qualities never emerged as vividly on-screen as they did in *Out of the Past*.

3. Harvey

1950, directed by Henry Koster. With James Stewart, Josephine Hull, Peggy Dow, Charles Drake, Cecil Kellaway, William H. Lynn, Victoria Horne, Jesse White

From the play (1944) by Mary Chase

Chase's play about an invisible (well, mostly invisible) six-foot white rabbit called Harvey and his pal, a good-natured drunk named Elwood P. Dowd, won a Pulitzer in 1945 and a Tony in 1948, but it wasn't until James Stewart played Elwood in the 1950 movie that this lithe little comedy really came to life. It's still pretty much a play on-screen, but the martini-drinking Elwood is the perfect vehicle for Stewart's bumbling, stumbling persona. For me, the best weapon in the world against ennui, depression, and most everything else life has to offer is simply to listen to Elwood's speech about how "nobody brings anything small into a bar." But it has to be Stewart speaking the words. Try it: you can't be bored if you're simultaneously laughing, crying, and making yourself a martini.

4. From Here to Eternity

1953, directed by Fred Zinneman. With Burt Lancaster, Montgomery Clift, Deborah Kerr, Donna Reed, Frank Sinatra, Ernest Borgnine, Philip Ober, Jack Warden

From the novel (1951) by James Jones

Jones's debut novel won the National Book Award and launched a distinguished career, though his later books never met with the same degree of success as this sprawling tale of the prewar Army in Hawaii, just prior to and immediately after the bombing of Pearl Harbor. It's a powerful, gripping book, but it's not without flaws. Jones's prose—like that of his hero, Thomas Wolfe—is a frustrating mix of eloquence and rhetorical bombast. He has great difficulty keeping himself out of his characters' dialogue, and he often belabors an idea as if it were an army boot that needed spit-shining. Zinneman's movie, written by Daniel Taradash, discards the bombast en masse and gives the dialogue back to the characters, who make the most of it: Montgomery Clift as the idealistic Private Robert E. Lee Prewitt ("I

Holly Golightly (Audrey Hepburn) is not a morning person, but her cat—named Cat—tries to wake her up anyway. *Breakfast at Tiffany's* expertly blends chic romance with comedy.

can soldier with any man"); Frank Sinatra (in his career-resurrecting role) as the tough but overmatched Maggio; Burt Lancaster as Sergeant Milt Warden, the wily noncom who steals the commanding officer's wife; and Deborah Kerr, as the wife. Oh, and there's a little make-out scene on the beach that you may have seen in a highlight reel or two. Good book but far, far better movie.

5. Breakfast at Tiffany's

1961, directed by Blake Edwards. With Audrey Hepburn, George Peppard, Patricia Neal, Buddy Ebsen, Martin Balsam, Mickey Rooney

From the novella (1958) by Truman Capote

This is a very tough call. Capote's novella is a jewel: utterly unsentimental in its portrayal of Holly Golightly (who really is a hooker in this version, no doubt about it) and boasting prose that's stiletto sharp and achingly eloquent. So why water that down, swapping hard-edged emotion for unabashed romance? Well, I guess because director Blake Edwards and writer George Axelrod realized that they'd been given Audrey Hepburn, Henry Mancini, and a little black dress, and those three elements, properly presented, could result in an iconic screen romance. No, the movie isn't exactly better than the book, but it is perhaps the ultimate example of changing the tone of a writer's work to produce something utterly different but completely wonderful in its own way. Let's just love them both and leave it at that.

6. Zorba the Greek

1964, directed by Michael Cacoyannis. With Anthony Quinn, Alan Bates, Irene Papas, Lila Kedrova, Sotiris Moustakas, Anna Kyriakou

From the novel (1952, English translation) by Nikos Kazantzakis

Another case of heavy-handed writing excised by a talented director, who, in this case, also wrote the screenplay. Philosophers rarely make great novelists, and Kazantzakis was more philosopher than fiction writer. He uses the Alan Bates character—Basil, a mopey Englishman—as a vehicle to deliver ponderous soliloquies on the melancholy nature of life, nearly drowning the story and forcing the book's triumphant character, Zorba—a life-loving, Falstaffian rogue—to fight for every scene. The movie tones down Basil and gives Zorba, perfectly portrayed by Anthony Quinn, all the room he needs to steal the show. Zorba at full cry is a cinematic treasure, capable of grinding philosophers and philosophy into sterile dust. Kazantzakis keeps his best character in check; Cacoyannis lets him wail.

7. The Godfather *and* The Godfather: Part II

1972 and 1974, directed by Francis Ford Coppola. With Al Pacino, Robert Duvall, Marlon Brando, Diane Keaton, Robert De Niro, Richard S. Castellano, Talia Shire, Morgana King, John Cazale, Sterling Hayden, John Marley

From the novel (1969) by Mario Puzo

This isn't as much of a no-brainer as one might think. Puzo's book is fine commercial fiction, a little pulpy (in a good way) with plenty of narrative drive and an unfailingly compelling cast of characters. The prose is a little rough around the edges, but that hardly gets in the way. So how did Coppola transform a thoroughly readable piece of grade-A pulp into two films that regularly appear at the top or near the top of every list of best movies ever?

Casting, of course, beginning with Brando and extending through the entire Corleone family and on down the list of supporting players (including the brilliant stroke of resurrecting film noir legend Sterling Hayden in the brief but indelible role of Captain McCluskey, the bent cop who takes two in the forehead from Michael Corleone). But not just casting. No one uses visual imagery better than Coppola did here to tell a story and to communicate subtle shades of meaning: the famous closing door at the end of Part I is but a single example, as Michael's transformation from idealistic soldier to ruthless mobster is complete, with Kay shut out completely. Then there is the use of light and dark in the Hollywood scenes—the bright, sunny, outdoor California landscape feeling so different from the claustrophobic, darkened rooms where the Corleones do their work in New York, so seemingly immune from the influence of overcoated mobsters. All an illusion, of course, and all a perfect setup for a horse's head in a movie mogul's bed. The list goes on and on, of course, in hundreds of books and thousands of film-student dissertations. It's simple really: in *The Godfather,* Coppola used the moviemaker's tools—cameras, lighting, music, sound—not merely to bring a story to life but to find new levels of meaning within that story.

8. Hopscotch

1980, directed by Ronald Neame. With Walter Matthau, Glenda Jackson, Sam Waterston, Ned Beatty, Herbert Lom

From the novel (1975) by Brian Garfield

Garfield's Edgar-winning novel is a fine book, but director Ronald Neame didn't let that stop him from doing a lot of fiddling. Fortunately, he's a good fiddler. Miles Kendig, an affable 50-something CIA agent, refuses to go out gently. He decides to extract his pound of flesh from the bureaucrats who run the agency by writing a memoir/exposé, which he mails, one chapter at a time, to the secret services of all the superpowers, who are soon enough chasing the wily agent across the globe as he hopscotches from country to country. The novel mixes high jinks with serious reflections on the spy trade, but in the movie version (cowritten, interestingly, by Garfield himself), the balance shifts decidedly in the direction of comedy—a recognition, perhaps, that Kendig, as portrayed by the inimitable Walter Matthau, could become the perfect laid-back, street-smart everyman to drive a jaunty caper flick. By playing to Matthau's strengths and adding Glenda Jackson as a love interest and sardonic foil, the filmmakers hit pay dirt. What really makes the comedic elements soar, however, is the movie's music. As Kendig capers about the Western world, he is accompanied by an irresistibly peppy classical music score. In perhaps the

> "Joe Cutter is tied to a chair in his room; you'd better cut him loose! . . . This is Eleanor Roosevelt."
> —MILES KENDIG, *HOPSCOTCH*

movie's signature set piece, Kendig booby-traps his boss's vacation home with firecrackers, and as the spooks attack the cottage with tear gas and gunfire, opera blares over rigged speakers (the comic version of Robert Duvall ravaging a Vietnamese village to a Wagnerian sound track in *Apocalypse Now*).

9. **Blade Runner**

1982, directed by Ridley Scott. With Harrison Ford, Rutger Hauer, Sean Young, Edward James Olmos, Daryl Hannah, M. Emmet Walsh, Brion James

From the novel Do Androids Dream of Electric Sheep? *(1968), by Philip K. Dick*

Legendary science-fiction writer Dick has his devotees, some of whom will surely be appalled to see *Blade Runner* on this list, but for my money, Scott's movie beats the novel easily. It's all in the visuals. Kudos to Dick for imagining a cyberpunk, noir-tinged LA where cars fly and hard-boiled PIs track down "replicants," but for those whose imaginations may not be quite as active as the author's, it really helps to see it. And Scott delivers fantastic pictures. It's significant that Dick was quoted as saying he imagined his world exactly as Scott filmed it. Scott, for his part, claims never to have read the book.

10. **Jaws**

1975, directed by Steven Spielberg. With Roy Scheider, Robert Shaw, Richard Dreyfuss, Lorraine Gary, Murray Hamilton

From the novel (1974) by Peter Benchley

It's scarier when you can see the shark—and Spielberg built himself a damn scary shark. End of story.

3

Gems from the National Film Registry of the Library of Congress

Established by the National Film Preservation Act of 1988, the National Film Registry of the Library of Congress identifies films that are culturally, historically, or aesthetically significant. Once every year the National Film Preservation Board announces additions to the list, which now includes more than five hundred movies. There are hundreds of well-known classics among them, such as *The Wizard of Oz, Casablanca, Star Wars,* and *Pinocchio,* as well as a multitude of treasures you might not recognize. Here are ten.

1. Newark Athlete (with Indian Clubs)

1891, produced by the Edison Manufacturing Company

A young man stands in front of a black background and performs a series of exercises. This fragment is both the oldest and (at twenty seconds) shortest film to be added to the Registry. It's available on *Edison: The Invention of the Movies,* a fascinating four-DVD set from Kino International that includes 140 complete films made between 1891 and 1918, all restored and featuring new musical scores. Watching them is akin to spying on the lifeforms of another planet; somehow the mere observation of simple human behavior in these films is nothing short of wondrous.

2. Let's All Go to the Lobby

1953, produced by Filmack Studios, Chicago

Another sweet short. Four anthropomorphic movie snacks dance down the aisle of a movie theater, cheerfully suggesting that now would be the perfect time to procure a treat. The popcorn "can't be beat"; furthermore, "the sparkling drinks are just dandy." Animated by Dave Fleischer, who also made the original Popeye cartoons, this short has set the tone for pretty much every cutesy in-theater ad since. Filmack has been producing film shorts since 1919—Walt Disney briefly worked there. You can find "Let's All Go to the Lobby" streaming on their website (www.filmack.com) and also on YouTube.

3. The Zapruder film

1963, filmed by Abraham Zapruder

Clothing manufacturer Zapruder had a fresh cartridge of Kodak Kodachrome II safety film in his 8 mm Bell and Howell Zoomatic Director Series Model 414 PD movie camera to capture President Kennedy's motorcade as it passed through Dealey Plaza in Dallas. The resulting film, made up of 486 frames (26.6 seconds), is probably the most famous home movie in history and remains the most complete visual document of Kennedy's assassination. The rather ghoulish documentary *Image of an Assassination: A New Look at the Zapruder Film* is an in-depth examination of the footage, even extracting visual information from the exposed film between the sprocket holes.

4. Laura

1944, directed by Otto Preminger. With Gene Tierney, Dana Andrews, Clifton Webb, Vincent Price, Judith Anderson, Dorothy Adams

It all starts with David Raksin's seductive theme music. Preminger uses it as a motif, an anchor for the central mystery: "Who killed Laura Hunt?" But that question is merely a device to lure us into contemplations of perversity amid the lushly decorated Manhattan interiors where the bulk of the action takes place. The dream settings that are the apartments of beautiful, stubborn career woman Laura Hunt and her mentor, acid-tongued gossip columnist Waldo Lydecker, are worlds as self-contained as the White Lodge and the Black Lodge in *Twin Peaks*. Little wonder,

> "I don't use a pen. I write with a goose quill dipped in venom."
>
> —WALDO LYDECKER, *LAURA*

Detective Mark McPherson (Dana Andrews) pines for a phantom in *Laura*. The ghostly portrait was actually a giant photograph touched up with paint.

then, that David Lynch borrowed several character names from *Laura* for his TV series. Repeat viewings of the movie only deepen the mystery. Is Waldo gay? Did Waldo and no-good gigolo Shelby Carpenter (a purringly oily Vincent Price) once have an affair? And the brilliant dialogue detaches itself further from the action: of Shelby, the elegant Mrs. Treadwell remarks, "He's no good, but he's what I want." The characters' behavior functions according to a weird, unknowable logic.

5. Touch of Evil

1958, directed by Orson Welles. With Charlton Heston, Orson Welles, Janet Leigh, Akim Tamiroff, Ray Collins, Dennis Weaver, Zsa Zsa Gabor, Marlene Dietrich, Mercedes McCambridge, Joseph Cotten

After a car bomb explosion in a sleazy town on the border, Mexican American detective Mike Vargas (Heston!) takes it upon himself to nab the culprit. But his investigation is thwarted at every turn by the corrupt, corpulent Captain Quinlan (Welles). Calling *Touch of Evil* a solid crime drama is like calling *The Maltese Falcon* a pretty good detective picture. It's a bravura display of technical wizardry, including the justly famous opening shot, a long take where the camera weaves around a line of cars at the border crossing. Welles populates the film with a rogue's gallery of grotesque characters (starting with himself), pumping up the atmosphere of sweaty paranoia. Henry Mancini's swingingly sinister latin rock score is tops. For more thoughts on Welles's use of sound, see chapter 4, "Extraordinary Sound, Music, and Film."

6. The French Connection

1971, directed by William Friedkin. With Gene Hackman, Roy Scheider, Fernando Rey, Tony Lo Bianco, Marcel Bozzuffi

Friedkin thrusts us into the middle of a hellish, grubby, chaotic New York City, as two detectives doggedly work toward intercepting a huge shipment of heroin. It's a movie that's influenced multiple generations of police thrillers, of course. But after all these years it's the little offhand details that really make the film feel so vivid. The bicycle in Hackman's apartment. Ugly wallpaper in an upper-class living room. A grape fountain drink in the subway. Nighttime steam rising from the pavement. Don Ellis's music score, rife with spooky horns and percussion, heightens the tension immensely, especially during a shootout in a dripping, ruined warehouse, which serves as an abrupt, almost existential ending.

7. A Woman under the Influence

1974, directed by John Cassavetes. With Gena Rowlands, Peter Falk, Fred Draper, Lady Rowlands, Katherine Cassavetes, Matthew Laborteaux, Matthew Cassel, Christina Grisanti

When his wife's erratic behavior deteriorates into a full-on mental breakdown, blue collar roughneck Nick is completely thrown for a loop. Can the two save their marriage? Perhaps Cassavetes's greatest achievement as an independent filmmaker, this raw slice of life exudes a loose, completely unpredictable sense of spontaneity (though in fact the film was very carefully scripted and rehearsed). As Mabel, the wife, Gena Rowlands gives a performance of almost unbearable intensity; and if you only know Peter Falk from *Columbo,* prepare yourself for a revelation.

8. El Norte

1983, directed by Gregory Nava. With Zaide Silvia Gutiérrez, David Villalpando, Ernesto Gómez Cruz, Lupe Ontiveros, Trinidad Silva, Enrique Castillo, Tony Plana, Diane Cary

Epic yet intimate, this intense saga follows the plight of Enrique and his sister Rosa as they flee war-torn Guatemala and immigrate illegally into the United States. In LA they work hard to achieve some kind of security, but threats ranging from the language barrier to deportation are always at their heels. Empathetic, moving, and surely still relevant to a whole range of issues we've scarcely begun to deal with in our society.

9. Harlan County, U.S.A.

1978 , directed by Barbara Kopple

A crew of men lie on their stomachs, riding a conveyor belt deep into the heart of a Kentucky coal mine, a cramped, filthy, dangerous place to work. To produce this landmark documentary, Kopple and her crew spent six years with the miners and their families who fought against the Eastover Mining Company (and its parent, Duke Energy) for better wages, benefits, and improved safety measures. There's an irony in watching those same men at risk of black lung from working in the mines spend their evenings in crowded, smoke-filled meeting halls. Giving the movie an extra charge is the ubiquitous presence of the miners' wives, right there alongside the men; their rugged determination not to fold is bracing.

10. Killer of Sheep

1978, directed by Charles Burnett. With Henry G. Sanders, Kaycee Moore, Charles Bracy, Angela Burnett, Eugene Cherry, Jack Drummond, Slim, Delores Farley

Kids chuck rocks at a passing train. Two thieves lift a TV set over an alley fence and under the disapproving gaze of a neighbor watering his lawn. The purchase of a car motor for $15 is considered at length. You can see some palm trees here and there, but you'd never know that Beverly Hills is only a half-hour's drive away. This is Watts. Burnett's film unfurls a handful of vignettes that vividly capture black life in the LA neighborhood. It's loosely wound around Stan, a sad-faced man who works at a local slaughterhouse, and his family. Grim it may be, but it's not without humor and charm. Shot by Burnett over a series of weekends with the help of friends, it was restored in 2007 by the UCLA Film and Television Archive and Milestone Films with financial assistance from Steven Soderbergh.

4

Extraordinary Sound, Music, and Film

By Ken Vandermark

Ken Vandermark is one of the most distinctive and influential jazz musicians playing and composing today. Based in Chicago since 1989, he has led or been a member of many groups, such as the celebrated Vandermark 5. He was awarded a MacArthur Fellowship in 1999. His music is featured on the soundtracks of two documentaries by Augusto Contento, *Roads of Water* and *Parallax Sounds*.

Rob's note > Since the advent of the talkies, cinema at its core has been about the melding of image and sound. When you stop to think about it, movies that successfully fuse the two into a perfect union—one where what you're seeing just wouldn't work without the soundtrack—are far from common. I asked Ken Vandermark, a guy who knows a thing or two about the power of sound, to write about some movies that pull it off; he also points out a few that don't.

1. Apocalypse Now

1979, directed by Francis Ford Coppola. With Martin Sheen, Marlon Brando, Robert Duvall, Laurence Fishburne, Dennis Hopper, Harrison Ford, Frederic Forrest, Sam Bottoms, Albert Hall

Though the *Redux* version Coppola released in 2001 has much extra and compelling footage, this is a rare case when I think the director's recut is weaker than the original release (unlike the example of Ridley Scott's *Blade Runner*). Sprawling and confused in the first version, adding more shorelines doesn't help motivate the narrative of the extended cut. The confusion works beautifully in the original, it's part of the fabric of the world Willard tries to survive, and the soundscape that Walter Murch developed and innovated for this journey is a cinematic landmark.

2. Ascenseur pour l'echafaud

1958, directed by Louis Malle. With Jeanne Moreau, Maurice Ronet, Georges Poujouly, Yori Bertin

Also known as *Elevator to the Gallows,* this film features a beautiful score composed by Miles Davis and performed with a mostly French ensemble (aside from the great Kenny Clarke on drums). The soundtrack anticipates Davis's classic album *Kind of Blue* by more than a year, and it introduces many new concepts Davis would further develop with John Coltrane, Bill Evans, et al. on the later recording. The story, acting, and Malle's direction are superb; one of the great combinations of jazz and film in cinema history.

3. Blacktop: A Story of the Washing of a School Play Yard

1952, directed by Charles and Ray Eames

All of the Eames films are fascinating, and taken collectively they give great insight into the thinking of two of the greatest designers of the twentieth century. This short movie, only eleven minutes long, is one of the strongest examples of how music can impact the way visual elements of a film are perceived. The concrete of a school lot is hosed clean to the strains of Bach's "Goldberg Variations," and it's absolutely mesmerizing. *Blacktop* is included in the DVD box-set *The Films of Charles and Ray Eames.*

4. A Clockwork Orange

1971, directed by Stanley Kubrick. With Malcolm McDowell, Godfrey Quigley, Anthony Sharp, Patrick Magee, Adrienne Corri, Warren Clarke, Michael Tarn, James Marcus

I think this is one of the most successful adaptations of a novel to the screen ever made; every nuance of Anthony Burgess's brutal and important book are effectively translated to film by Kubrick's direction. Wendy Carlos (then Walter Carlos) does something similar with the soundtrack. She rearranges some of the most famous compositions from the history of classical music, particularly the themes of Beethoven, by using the Moog synthesizer, transforming the source material in ways that are true to the original and also true to the electronic instrument. I think Kubrick is one of the few directors who really understands music and how to use its power in a visual context. His choice of the score for *A Clockwork*

Orange, the way it interacts and represents the film's subject matter, is a testament to this aspect of his genius.

5. The Conversation

1974, directed by Francis Ford Coppola. With Gene Hackman, John Cazale, Allen Garfield, Cindy Williams, Frederic Forrest, Harrison Ford, Robert Duvall

Back to Coppola. There are superficial parallels between this film and Michelangelo Antonioni's 1966 movie, *Blow-Up*: the first is about trying to fully understand what you hear; the second is about trying to fully understand what you see—and both movies are about the failure to do so. In addition to a great performance by Gene Hackman, *The Conversation* contains the most complete investigation of sound within a narrative film, how it communicates and how it doesn't, that I've ever seen.

Gene Hackman as obsessive sound engineer Harry Caul in *The Conversation,* a movie that examines the difference between just hearing something and listening to it.

Akim Tamiroff and Orson Welles in *Touch of Evil*. Between the ravishing nocturnal look of the movie and the densely layered soundtrack, it's truly a feast for the senses.

6. Touch of Evil

1958, directed by Orson Welles. With Charlton Heston, Orson Welles, Janet Leigh, Akim Tamiroff, Ray Collins, Dennis Weaver, Zsa Zsa Gabor, Marlene Dietrich, Mercedes McCambridge, Joseph Cotten

There is so much misfortune and misunderstanding connected to Welles's career; thankfully there are lasting examples of his genius that supersede the melodrama of his life. The restored version of *Touch of Evil* is one of them. Yes, there is the famous beginning; yes, there is a great score by Henry Mancini; but perhaps the most amazing thing about this film is Welles's use of sound. The ending radio sequence with Charlton Heston and Welles himself is as much a tour de force as the film's legendary opening shot. (*Rob's note:* For more thoughts on *Touch of Evil,* see chapter 3, "Gems from the National Film Registry of the Library of Congress.")

7. The Good, the Bad, and the Ugly

1966, directed by Sergio Leone. With Clint Eastwood, Lee Van Cleef, Eli Wallach, Antonio Casale, Al Mulock

Ennio Morricone is rightfully considered to be one of the great soundtrack composers in history. My favorite Morricone composition is "Invenzione per John" from *Duck, You Sucker!* but I think that this is his most completely successful score. It's also one of my favorite films—a rare, perfect synthesis between sight and sound: story, direction, acting, score.

8. Hunger

2008, directed by Steve McQueen.
With Michael Fassbender, Liam Cunningham,
Liam McMahon, Stuart Graham, Brian
Milligan, Laine Megaw, Karen Hassan

9. Shame

2011, directed by Steve McQueen.
With Michael Fassbender, Carey Mulligan,
Nicole Beharie, James Badge Dale, Hannah
Ware, Robert Montano, Lucy Walters

Let me compare these two films by Steve McQueen. I think *Hunger* is one of the best films from the first decade of the twenty-first century (fitting for my piece here, it was recommended to me by another musician—Jason Moran). It is structurally perfect; every element counts and carries equal weight. And other than the ambient sound in each scene, there is almost no soundtrack; only a few moments of music are used toward the very end of the movie. McQueen's second narrative film, *Shame,* utilizes a more conventional, Hollywood-style score. The music tells the audience how to feel about each event, and the movie is much weaker because of this erasure of ambiguity.

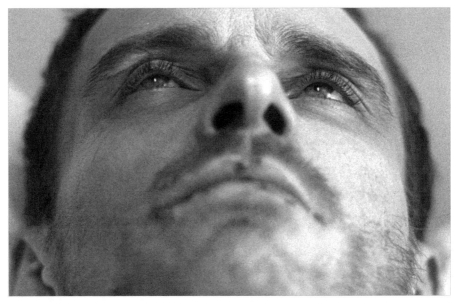

Michael Fassbender in *Hunger*. To play IRA member Bobby Sands, who goes on a hunger strike in prison, Fassbender went on a medically monitored diet of berries, nuts, and sardines.

10. The Cook, the Thief, His Wife, and Her Lover

1989, directed by Peter Greenaway. With Richard Bohringer, Michael Gambon, Helen Mirren, Alan Howard, Tim Roth, Ciarán Hinds

Greenaway is one of the most innovative directors overlapping the twentieth and twenty-first centuries. This film is compelling, inscrutable, and visually extraordinary. Yet, why is it that so many forward-thinking contemporary artists have such regressive taste in music? Michael Nyman's faux-Baroque score is shallow and excruciating, particularly a theme that's repeatedly sung by a young boy. Maybe even Greenaway became tired of this material—two characters in the story actually ask the boy to stop singing!

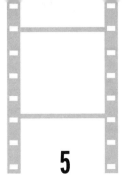

5

Seven Reasons to Love Nicolas Cage

By Zoe Trope

Zoe Trope is the author of *Please Don't Kill the Freshman,* a memoir of her high school years published when she was 17 years old. She graduated from Emporia State University's School of Library and Information Management in 2010. She lives in Portland, Oregon, and enjoys many other films that do not star Nicolas Cage.

I was born in 1986. A year later, Nicolas Cage starred in his biggest role to date in *Moonstruck,* a movie that my family owned on VHS tape. As a child, I watched it over and over again (something about Cher slapping him in the face and telling him to "Snap out of it!" always electrified me) and have been in love with Nicolas Cage ever since. I hope you are, too.

1. The Rock

1996, directed by Michael Bay. With Nicolas Cage, Sean Connery, Ed Harris, Michael Biehn, William Forsythe, David Morse, John Spencer, Vanessa Marcil

Nicolas Cage is the nerdy, beige-Volvo-driving biochemist with a pregnant wife at home who saunters into work one day to find a hostage situation with chemical weapons at Alcatraz sitting on his desk. Sean Connery keeps a firm grip on the spotlight as the only man who has ever escaped Alcatraz (dramatic music cue) but

27

occasionally shares the audience's attention with Cage. This movie has lots of explosions and corny lines, along with Sean Connery's spine-tingling accent. It's everything great about action flicks.

2. Con Air

1997, directed by Simon West. With Nicolas Cage, John Cusack, John Malkovich, Monica Potter, Ving Rhames, Mykelti Williamson, Nick Chinlund, Rachel Ticotin, Steve Buscemi

The mid-'90s were a good time for Nicolas Cage to play the unwitting hero with a pregnant wife. In this one, as Cameron Poe, he accidentally kills a dude who was trying to rough up Poe's mama-to-be and is sentenced to seven years in prison. Upon his release, he ends up in a plane full of crazies and has to save the day. His hair is long and his face is sad, but we love him anyway.

> "Dr. Walsh! I was just enjoying some of your Greatest Hits here. Oh, I hope you don't mind, I partook in your groovy painkillers."
>
> –CASTOR TROY, FACE/OFF

3. Face/Off

1997, directed by John Woo. With Nicolas Cage, John Travolta, Joan Allen, Alessandro Nivola, Gina Gershon, Dominique Swain, Nick Cassavetes, C. C. H. Pounder, Margaret Cho

Nicolas Cage is the bad guy, Castor Troy, whose face is taken off and put on John Travolta. Not sure who got the worse end of the deal here, but keep your disbelief fully suspended during this 138-minute crazy train driven by John Woo.

4. Moonstruck

1987, directed by Norman Jewison. With Nicolas Cage, Cher, Olympia Dukakis, Vincent Gardenia, Danny Aiello, Julie Bovasso, Louis Guss, John Mahoney

Nicolas Cage is Ronny, the one-handed Brooklyn baker whose brother, Johnny, is engaged to the beautiful big-haired Loretta, played by Cher. In their first meeting, Ronny tells Loretta the story of losing his hand in a bread slicer because Johnny distracted him, and he implores her, "I want you to watch me kill myself so you can tell my brother on his wedding day." What a charmer! Romance ensues.

5. Ghost Rider

2007, directed by Mark Steven Johnson. With Nicolas Cage, Eva Mendes, Wes Bentley, Sam Elliott, Donal Logue, Peter Fonda

Nicolas Cage is Johnny Blaze, a motorcycle-riding guy who made a deal with the devil because his dad was sick and now sometimes his skull is engulfed in flames.

When he's not busy saving hostages from chemical weapons, Stanley Goodspeed (Nicolas Cage) likes to relax by strumming his guitar. One of the few quiet moments in *The Rock*, directed with jaw-dropping bombast by Michael Bay.

Apparently he has to fight the devil's son or something? We're not sure. But Eva Mendes makes out with him.

6. Lord of War

2005, directed by Andrew Niccol. With Nicolas Cage, Jared Leto, Bridget Moynahan, Ethan Hawke, Eamonn Walker, Ian Holm

Nicolas Cage is Yuri Orlov, a rapacious arms dealer who profits from conflict and killing around the globe. The film was written and directed by Andrew Niccol, the twisty-turny mind behind *The Truman Show* and *Gattaca* (and a film for which he must be forgiven for writing, *The Terminal*—that ridiculous rom-com with Tom Hanks and Catherine Zeta-Jones). Cage's relationship with his younger brother, played by Jared Leto, forces him to confront the immorality of his chosen profession.

7. Adaptation.

2002, directed by Spike Jonze. With Nicolas Cage, Meryl Streep, Chris Cooper, Cara Seymour, Tilda Swinton, Brian Cox, Maggie Gyllenhaal, Judy Greer

Nicolas Cage is simultaneously Charlie Kaufman and Donald Kaufman, a real man and an imagined one. Screenwriter Charlie Kaufman is attempting to adapt Susan Orlean's *The Orchid Thief,* a book about flowers and swamps and obsession. Cage as C. Kaufman is fat and sweaty and self-loathing; Cage as the fictional D. Kaufman is manic, childish, and obnoxious; Meryl Streep as Orlean is probing, lonely, and breathtakingly beautiful. While this list is an ode to the bizarrely flexible Cage, I have to say that this movie is worth it just for the scene where Streep harmonizes with a dial tone.

6

Psycho, and Other Surprising Christmastime Movies

The list of traditional yuletide classics is a long one. *It's A Wonderful Life, A Christmas Story,* and *Elf* would all make the cut. But there's a whole other group of movies that happen to take place in late December, consciously or unconsciously using a Christmastime setting to ironic effect.

1. Psycho

1960, directed by Alfred Hitchcock. With Anthony Perkins, Janet Leigh, Vera Miles, John Gavin, Martin Balsam

Just after the famous opening credits, designed by Saul Bass, we're treated to a panorama of the Phoenix skyline before the camera slowly moves into a hotel room where a tawdry affair between secretary Marion Crane (Leigh) and Sam Loomis (Gavin) is unfolding. Establishing titles give the time and place: "Phoenix, Arizona," then "Friday, December the eleventh." Why did Hitchcock insert these identifiers? The reason is rather prosaic: when the second unit footage was being shot, it happened to be Chistmastime, and Hitchcock didn't want the audience to be confused or distracted by the holiday decorations that can be seen in the back-

31

What's in that envelope? *Psycho* brilliantly illustrates Hitchcock's skillful method of creating suspense: letting the audience know something a character doesn't.

ground of several shots. Interestingly, the notorious shower sequence was also shot during Christmastime, from December 17 to December 23, 1959.

2. Rosemary's Baby

1968, directed by Roman Polanski. With Mia Farrow, John Cassavetes, Ruth Gordon, Sidney Blackmer, Maurice Evans, Ralph Bellamy, Charles Grodin

Polanski's shocker a Christmas movie? Indeed. In one scene, the pregnant Rosemary kills some time waiting for her friend Hutch by looking at a department store's Christmas windows. But he never shows. The creepy music on the soundtrack tips us off that all is not well—Hutch has been stricken by a satanic curse after finding out the truth about Rosemary's sinister neighbors.

3. Die Hard

1988, directed by John McTiernan. With Bruce Willis, Alan Rickman, Bonnie Bedelia, Alexander Godunov, Reginald VelJohnson, Paul Gleason, De'voreaux White, William Atherton

NYPD officer John McClane picks the wrong highrise office Christmas party to crash: it's about to be commandeered by high-stakes thieves masquerading as terrorists. Get a load of the sleigh bells Michael Kamen slyly works into his score. This high-octane action movie features a terrific script and direction, not to mention Bruce Willis's best performance to date. Also plenty of quaint period details such as wearing a gun on an airplane, smoking in the airport, and references to Yasser Arafat.

4. The Silent Partner

1978, directed by Daryl Duke. With Elliott Gould, Christopher Plummer, Susannah York, John Candy

Die Hard wasn't the first suspense thriller set during the holidays. Shortly before Christmas, when shopping mall bank teller Miles Cullen (Gould) gets wind of a planned robbery hatched by an ersatz Santa Claus (Plummer), he takes steps to divert some of the loot for himself. Once the bank robber realizes he's been had, a game of wits ensues. Gould's laconic attitude is the perfect foil for Plummer's flamboyant psycho. The bracing moments of brutal violence are courtesy of scripter Curtis Hanson, who would later direct *The Hand That Rocks the Cradle* and *L.A. Confidential.*

5. The Thin Man

1934, directed by W. S. Van Dyke. With William Powell, Myrna Loy, Maureen O'Sullivan, Nat Pendleton, Minna Gombell, Cesar Romero, Porter Hall

Crime and Christmas go hand in hand. While relaxing in their deluxe hotel suite over the Christmas holidays, sophisticated sleuths Nick and Nora Charles find themselves embroiled in a murder mystery. An incomparable classic that's enjoyable no matter what time of year it is, it features a memorable scene where Nora lounges around on Christmas morning in pajamas and fur coat. Meanwhile, Nick tests out his new BB gun on some Christmas tree ornaments. Isn't that the kind of Christmas morning we've all fantasized about?

6. Bad Santa

2003, directed by Terry Zwigoff. With Billy Bob Thornton, Tony Cox, Brett Kelly, Lauren Graham, Lauren Tom, John Ritter, Bernie Mac

There's subtle and there's . . . *Bad Santa.* Thornton has one of his best roles as a foul-mouthed drunken Santa who, with the help of a dwarf, loots the shopping malls where he works. This raunchy crime comedy gleefully trashes all the yuletide trappings, from sex with Santa to shotgun blasting nativity figurines. But a subplot involving a lonely kid just goes to show that even under vicious assault, the Christmas spirit is pretty darn resilient. Ritter, in his last film, has some choice moments as a suspicious mall manager.

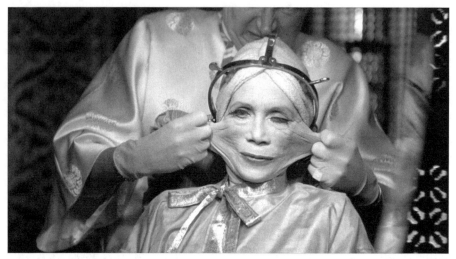

Ida Lowry (Katherine Helmond) treats herself to radical plastic surgery over the Christmas holidays. Wacky and disturbing, *Brazil* remains Terry Gilliam's best movie.

7. Brazil

1985, directed by Terry Gilliam. With Jonathan Pryce, Kim Greist, Robert De Niro, Katherine Helmond, Ian Holm, Bob Hoskins, Michael Palin

Santa Claus asks the little boy sitting on his lap what he'd like for Christmas. He replies, "My own credit card." Blending Charles Dickens, *A Clockwork Orange,* and *1984,* this dystopian black comedy about the intersection of consumerism and terrorism is a tour de force by Monty Python's Gilliam. De Niro excels in a small role as a guerrilla heating engineer, and Michael Kamen's catchy score (which often appears in movie trailers these days) cleverly incorporates the standard tune that shares the film's title.

8. Eyes Wide Shut

1999, directed by Stanley Kubrick. With Tom Cruise, Nicole Kidman, Sydney Pollack, Marie Richardson, Todd Field, Rade Šerbedžija, Leelee Sobieski, Alan Cumming

The colorful holiday lights that appear in nearly every scene add a surrealistic flavor to this dreamlike examination of sexual obsession and jealousy. Kubrick uses the festive trappings of the season as a counterpoint to the icy and awkward encounters depicted on-screen, as Dr. William Harford and his wife Alice find their marriage threatened by secrets both real and imagined. The film's startling final scene takes place in a busy toy store.

9. Tuesday, after Christmas

2010, directed by Radu Muntean. With Maria Popistaşu, Mimi Brănescu, Mirela Oprişor, Dragoş Bucur, Victor Rebengiuc

Most movies on the subject of divorce eagerly present simple, straightforward reasons for the dissolution of a marriage. "If only couple A hadn't done X, Y, or Z," the thinking goes, "they'd still be together." But real life isn't like that. Paul and Adriana, the husband and wife at the center of this movie, have been married long enough to create and maintain a stable, upper-middle-class existence. They both have successful careers, a circle of friends, and a beautiful daughter together. From the way we see them kid each other while shopping for a snowboard for their little daughter's Christmas present, it's clear there's genuine affection between them—they care for each other, and they're comfortable together. But Paul has fallen in love with another woman, a dentist named Raluca, and it's equally certain that she loves him. Things finally come to a boil around the holidays, when he realizes that a reckoning cannot be put off any longer. This searing portrait of disintegration uses long takes and naturalistic sound and acting to place us in a recognizable reality that's quietly devastating.

> "You've made a rag of me."
>
> —RALUCA, *TUESDAY, AFTER CHRISTMAS*

7

Twelve Films That Made Me Love America

By Bilge Ebiri

Bilge Ebiri was born in York, England, lived in Turkey with his parents until the age of 7, and then emigrated to the United States. In 2003, he wrote, directed, and coproduced the feature film *New Guy*. He has written about film for numerous publications, including *New York Magazine*, Moving Image Source, the *New York Sun*, *Time Out New York*, *Minneapolis City Pages*, and nerve.com. His essay "The Disloyal Bunch" was included in the Criterion release of *Three Outlaw Samurai*.

I became a US citizen a couple of years ago. Don't ask me why it took so long. I had a green card for something like twenty-five years, and I always knew I'd eventually become a real citizen. Along the way certain films would reinforce that desire. I'm not talking about the kind of macho fantasies that pass for patriotic movies. I'm talking about films that convey America's many complexities, while still somehow managing to reaffirm my love for it. Indeed, many of these films might be deemed unpatriotic by some people. To those people I say, "*Phffft.*" Here are twelve films that made me want to become an American.

1. All the President's Men

1976, directed by Alan J. Pakula. With Robert Redford, Dustin Hoffman, Jason Robards, Jack Warden, Hal Holbrook, Jane Alexander

The Watergate scandal may have led to some sort of crisis of confidence for the country, but if you think about it, it was also one of our finer hours—in which the most controlling and corrupt executive in modern US history was brought down by the perseverance and independence of two ordinary reporters who refused to be cowed by threatening displays of power. Some on the Right may try to claim a monopoly on American-ness, but Woodward (birthplace: Geneva, Illinois) and Bernstein (birthplace: Washington, DC), at least as depicted in this film, are pretty much the working definition of American heroes.

2. Amistad

1997, directed by Steven Spielberg. With Morgan Freeman, Anthony Hopkins, Djimon Hounsou, Matthew McConaughey, Nigel Hawthorne, Stellan Skarsgård, Harry Blackmun, Anna Paquin

"And if it means civil war? Then let it come. And when it does, may it be, finally, the last battle of the American Revolution."

3. The Best Years of Our Lives

1946, directed by William Wyler. With Fredric March, Myrna Loy, Dana Andrews, Teresa Wright, Virginia Mayo, Harold Russell

William Wyler's epic about the many challenges—physical, marital, professional, and other—faced by soldiers returning from World War II most definitely struck a chord with a newly victorious nation, winning eight Oscars and making a mint at the box office (though that didn't stop some from hilariously accusing it of Communist propaganda; apparently they objected to the portrayal of some bankers). Wyler gets little credit for being a stylist, but his use of deep focus here is on par with anything in *Citizen Kane*. (It helps, too, that Gregg Toland shot this.) But that's not why this film is on my list. The sensitive and subtle portrayal of its veteran heroes—somewhat surprising, given the gung-ho zeitgeist of the times—hasn't dated one bit. Not everybody agrees: Andrew Sarris, displaying his usual allergy toward movies that actually achieve what they set out to accomplish, once labeled it "humanitarian blackmail."

4. Born on the Fourth of July

1989, directed by Oliver Stone. With Tom Cruise, Kyra Sedgwick, Raymond J. Barry, Jerry Levine, Frank Whaley, Willem Dafoe

In case you weren't sure, that title is in fact meant to be ironic. Oliver Stone's masterpiece follows Ron Kovic (Cruise) from his youthful days as a rah-rah All-American jock through the crucible of Vietnam to his emergence as a paraplegic antiwar protester. But that journey of disillusionment is mirrored by one of self-awakening, as Kovic discovers the power of his own voice. Example: Stone shoots

Kovic's disruption of the 1972 Republican National Convention (and subsequent hauling off by security while fresh-faced Nixon Youth spit vitriol at him) like it was the parting of the Red Sea. Perhaps because it's a journey Stone himself knows something about—having gone from writing fascist drivel like *Conan the Barbarian* to becoming the country's foremost chronicler of its stray ideals.

5. Brewster McCloud

1970, directed by Robert Altman. With Bud Cort, Sally Kellerman, Michael Murphy, William Windom, Shelley Duvall, Rene Auberjonois, Margaret Hamilton, Stacy Keach, John Schuck

6. Nashville

1975, directed by Robert Altman. With Barbara Baxley, Ned Beatty, Karen Black, Ronee Blakley, Keith Carradine, Geraldine Chaplin, Robert DoQui, Shelley Duvall, Allen Garfield, Henry Gibson, Scott Glenn, Jeff Goldblum, Barbara Harris, David Hayward, Michael Murphy, Allan F. Nicholls, Cristina Raines, Bert Remsen, Lily Tomlin, Gwen Welles, and Keenan Wynn

A bona fide war hero who picked apart the darkest corners of his country's soul like they were the wings of a well-boiled chicken, Robert Altman was quite possibly the most American of directors. Sure, the patriotic pageantry on display in these two films is tongue-in-cheek, but look at their boisterously freewheeling narratives, their constantly dreaming characters, their poisonous sarcasm, their hauntingly corrosive finales, and tell me these movies could have existed in any other country but this one. (Not that the country noticed, but still.)

7. The Godfather: Part II

1974, directed by Francis Ford Coppola. With Al Pacino, Robert Duvall, Diane Keaton, Robert De Niro, Talia Shire, Morgana King, John Cazale

I suppose there's something perverse about including a film that makes the corruption of the American Dream its oft-stated subject, but Coppola's film is also, as it so happens, the most powerful depiction of said dream that I've seen, particularly in its flashbacks to Vito Corleone's earlier years. [*Rob's note:* For another appreciation, see chapter 2, "Better Than the Book!"]

8. The Long Gray Line

1955, directed by John Ford. With Tyrone Power, Maureen O'Hara, Robert Francis, Donald Crisp, Ward Bond, Betsy Palmer

John Ford's look at the life of an Irish immigrant (Power) who started off as a dishwasher at West Point and wound up spending decades at the military academy (later working in the athletics department) is the kind of borderline jingoistic film I can actually get behind—tender, boisterous, and almost unbearably human. It's one of the more gentle military movies you'll ever see, perhaps because it doesn't have any real war scenes. Not as "deep," perhaps, as the best of Ford's cavalry films, but it does feel like the purest distillation of this particular director's genuine patriotism.

9. Manhattan

1979, directed by Woody Allen. With Woody Allen, Diane Keaton, Michael Murphy, Mariel Hemingway, Meryl Streep, Anne Byrne, Wallace Shawn

> "She's 17. I'm 42 and she's 17. I'm older than her father, can you believe that? I'm dating a girl, wherein, I can beat up her father."
>
> —ISAAC DAVIS, MANHATTAN

The idea that one of his films might make someone proud to be an American would probably send Woody Allen into a fit of nonstop vomiting, but I must insist. Everybody of course remembers that opening voiceover, in which Isaac Davis (Allen) tries out opening lines to his novel. It's clear he loves New York—"He adored New York City" is more often than not the first sentence. But he keeps wanting to delve into its flaws, to undercut his love ("To him it was a metaphor for the decay of contemporary culture," "He romanticized it all out of proportion," etc.). He finally settles on acceptance: "New York was his town, and it always would be." That opening mirrors the trajectory of the film itself: "Boy, this is really a great city," our resident cynic later says. "I don't care what anybody says. It's really a knockout." What does that have to do with loving one's country? Everything, when you think about it—especially since, as someone once said, "New York is the America Factory."

10. The New World

2005, directed by Terrence Malick. With Colin Farrell, Q'orianka Kilcher, Christopher Plummer, Christian Bale

I know. Malick. Of course. *The New World* isn't about Indians and settlers so much as it is about salvation. Pocahontas saves the fallen dreamer John Smith, only to be saved herself in her moment of disgrace by the patient, practical John Rolfe, setting up their subdued love triangle as a kind of romantic dialectic between idealism and pragmatism—which also (surprise!) happen to be the twin poles of the American experience. In its own audacious, iconoclastic way, *The New World* returns hope to one of our founding myths. It dares to suggest that the nation was borne not of blood, violence, and persecution, but of romantic redemption and a love that passeth understanding.

One of the beauties of Terrence Malick's *The New World* is the way it makes early America feel like a completely foreign country, which by extension helps the audience see contemporary America with fresh eyes.

11. Team America: World Police

2004, directed by Trey Parker. With Trey Parker, Matt Stone, Kristen Miller, Masasa, Daran Norris, Phil Hendrie, Maurice LaMarche

It pretty much goes against everything I just wrote, but I'd be lying if I didn't put this on this list.

12. Waking the Dead

2000, directed by Keith Gordon. With Billy Crudup, Jennifer Connelly, Molly Parker, Janet McTeer, Paul Hipp, Sandra Oh, Hal Holbrook

Again: Odd, perhaps, to include a movie that opens with its heroine being blown away by what is probably a CIA car bomb, but Keith Gordon's way, way under-rated film about the romance between a headstrong activist (Connelly) and a straight-arrow conservative Coast Guard officer (Crudup) does one of the best jobs I've ever seen of portraying the way Americans of sharply different political stripes can not only get along but directly influence each other, even from beyond the grave: in the film's contemporary storyline, Crudup's character, now a politician, loses and regains his soul as he's haunted by the spectral presence of his idealistic late paramour.

8

Nine Westerns
That Aren't Westerns

The Western is both a genre and a state of mind, and infinitely flexible. Since the age of silent Western heroes like William S. Hart, who was parodied by Buster Keaton in his 1922 movie *The Frozen North,* filmmakers have delighted in transplanting the elements of the traditional Western into a variety of stories and locales. Here are nine such specimens.

1. Seven Samurai

1954, directed by Akira Kurosawa. With Toshirô Mifune, Takashi Shimura, Keiko Tsushima, Yukiko Shimazaki, Kamatari Fujiwara, Daisuke Katô, Isao Kimura, Minoru Chiaki

Possibly the most famous "transplanted Western" of all. A ragtag bunch of warriors join forces to protect a village from marauding invaders. Kurosawa's peerless adventure movie was inspired by Hollywood Westerns; Hollywood returned the favor by refashioning it into *The Magnificent Seven.* Breathtaking action set pieces mixed with moments of wry comedy form a template that's still being used in today's summer blockbusters.

Toshirô Mifune in *Seven Samurai:* the ultimate warrior in the ultimate Western from the Far East.

2. Meek's Cutoff

2010, directed by Kelly Reichardt. With Michelle Williams, Paul Dano, Bruce Greenwood,
Shirley Henderson, Neal Huff, Zoe Kazan, Tommy Nelson, Will Patton

The year is 1845 and the place is the desert wilderness of eastern Oregon, somewhere on the Oregon Trail. But there are no gunfights, no saloons, no cowboys,
and no whorehouses in this Western. Just a group of pioneer settlers, ordinary
folks trying to make a new life for themselves at the mercy of an indifferent environment and their own doubts, struggling to make their way to a paradise they
feel awaits them. Reichardt and screenwriter Jon Raymond take a hackneyed
genre and strip away all the clichés, showing with an extraordinary intimacy a
world that feels completely alien: an existence where the most sophisticated piece
of technology is a hand-cranked coffee grinder, and you repair your vehicle's
chassis by chopping a log to the proper dimensions.

3. Mad Max

1979, directed by George Miller. With Mel Gibson, Steve Bisley, Joanne Samuel, Hugh Keays-Byrne,
Tim Burns, Geoff Parry

A loner crisscrosses the desolate countryside, searching for the thugs who murdered
his wife and child in order to exact vengeance. The setting is dystopian Australia;
and instead of using horses to get around, the modes of transportation are tricked-

out cars and motorcycles. When it was first released, the US distributors had Mel Gibson's voice dubbed by an American actor—they figured that audiences would find his Australian accent distracting!

4. Duel

1971, directed by Steven Spielberg. With Dennis Weaver, Jacqueline Scott, Carey Loftin, Eddie Firestone, Lou Frizzell, Eugene Dynarski, Lucille Benson

> "It's that rat circus out there, I'm beginning to enjoy it. Look, any longer out on that road and I'm one of them, a terminal psychotic, except that I've got this bronze badge that says that I'm one of the good guys."
>
> —MAX ROCKATANSKY, *MAD MAX*

While driving solo through the desert, harried businessman Weaver makes the mistake of passing a malevolent trucker on the highway. Soon the two are engaged in a dangerous game of cat-and-mouse road rage. Screenwriter Richard Matheson, who wrote many unforgettable episodes of *The Twilight Zone,* updates the trope of the climactic shootout for the auto age. Shot in only thirteen days by 24-year-old Spielberg, *Duel* is a classic of minimalist suspense that points the way toward moments in later blockbusters such as *Jaws* and *Raiders of the Lost Ark.*

5. Brother

2000, directed by Takeshi Kitano. With Takeshi Kitano, Omar Epps, Claude Maki, Tetsuya Watari, Masaya Kato, Susumu Terajima, Royale Watkins, Lombardo Boyar

West meets East in this violent urban yarn. Following a bad situation in Japan, a Yakuza hit man flees to LA. There, he hooks up with his half-brother, and before long they decide to take over and streamline one of the local drug rings. Writer/director/star Kitano's stoically powerful action flick is loaded with uneasy tension that periodically erupts in gunfire, making a point of showing the consequences of violence.

6. Outland

1981, directed by Peter Hyams. With Sean Connery, Peter Boyle, Frances Sternhagen, James Sikking, Kika Markham, Clarke Peters, Steven Berkoff

Newly appointed federal marshal Connery comes to town, sizes up the rampant corruption on display, and decides he doesn't like it. What's to do but clean house? Only in this case the town is a mining colony on one of Jupiter's moons. While not exactly a underrated gem, *Outland* is a pulpy good time with plenty of "advanced" early '80s technology on-screen. Boyle is impressively slimy as the bad guy who eventually gets his just desserts, and Sternhagen shines as an acerbic doctor.

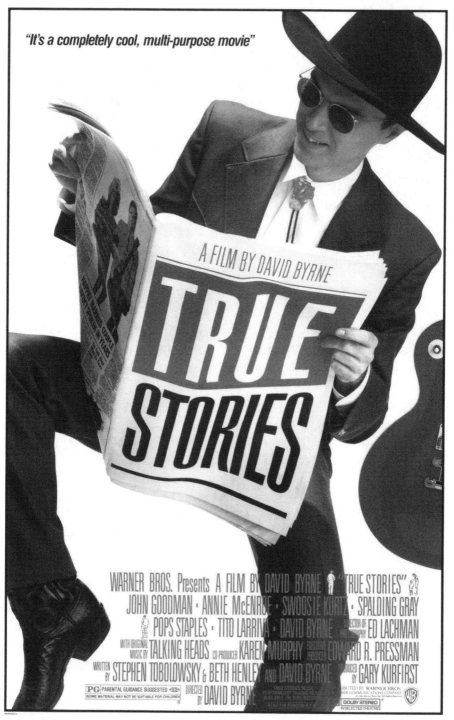

"It's a completely cool, multi-purpose movie"

A FILM BY DAVID BYRNE

TRUE STORIES

WARNER BROS. Presents A FILM BY DAVID BYRNE "TRUE STORIES"
JOHN GOODMAN · ANNIE McENROE · SWOOSIE KURTZ · SPALDING GRAY
POPS STAPLES · TITO LARRIVA · DAVID BYRNE DIRECTOR OF PHOTOGRAPHY ED LACHMAN
WITH ORIGINAL MUSIC BY TALKING HEADS CO-PRODUCER KAREN MURPHY EXECUTIVE PRODUCER EDWARD R. PRESSMAN
WRITTEN BY STEPHEN TOBOLOWSKY & BETH HENLEY AND DAVID BYRNE PRODUCED BY GARY KURFIRST
PG PARENTAL GUIDANCE SUGGESTED
SOME MATERIAL MAY NOT BE SUITABLE FOR CHILDREN
DIRECTED BY DAVID BYRNE
DOLBY STEREO
IN SELECTED THEATRES

I was 13 when I saw *True Stories*. It was the first time I realized that a movie could do more than just tell a story.

46

7. Quintet

1979, directed by Robert Altman. With Paul Newman, Vittorio Gassman, Fernando Rey,
Bibi Andersson, Brigitte Fossey, Nina Van Pallandt, Craig Richard Nelson

In a frozen world of the future, the survivors of a devastated city while away the time playing a complicated game of strategy called Quintet. Into this setting venture a taciturn hunter (Newman) and his pregnant wife. They soon learn that the stakes of *Quintet* are very high indeed. Possibly both Altman and Newman's most unloved movie, this enigmatic tale was conceived of as a "glacial Western." And the snail-like pacing has definitely been known to put viewers to sleep. But striking production design (it was filmed in the icy ruins of Montreal's Expo '67 pavilion) and a genuinely odd atmosphere make it worth a look for the curious.

8. Survival of the Dead

2009, directed by George A. Romero. With Alan Van Sprang, Kenneth Welsh, Kathleen Munroe,
Devon Bostick, Richard Fitzpatrick, Athena Karkanis, Stefano Di Matteo, Joris Jarsky

Romero's sixth zombie movie has the structure of a classic Western: two rival clans who have been at odds for as long as anyone can remember are forced to deal with the presence of strangers in their midst—in this case, a small band of people fleeing the zombie hordes. Amidst the expertly staged scenes of gory horror Romero even finds time for a climactic shootout (in this case, the O.K. Corral serves as a pen for zombies).

9. True Stories

1986, directed by David Byrne. With David Byrne, John Goodman, Swoosie Kurtz, Spalding Gray, Pops
Staples, Tito Larriva, Jo Harvey Allen, John Ingle

Cowriter/director/narrator (and Talking Heads frontman) Byrne takes us on a tour of Virgil, Texas, a small town preparing for a "Celebration of Specialness" in honor of Texas's sesquicentennial. Largely jettisoning a straightforward story, *True Stories* is a collection of deadpan comic vignettes, weird ideas, musical numbers, and observations about Reagan-era America inspired by *Weekly World News*–style tabloid articles. It's about shopping malls, highways, technology, conspiracy theories, religion, and even love. In other words, it captures 1986 perfectly. The soundtrack includes songs performed both by Talking Heads and various actors in the film (the track "Radio Head" inspired a certain well-known band)—John Goodman even croons a country tune.

9

Tropical Cocktails at the Movies

By Jeff "Beachbum" Berry

One of *Imbibe* magazine's "25 Most Influential Cocktail Personalities of the Past Century," Jeff "Beachbum" Berry is the author of five books on vintage tiki drinks and cuisine, which *Los Angeles* magazine has called "the keys to the tropical kingdom." He's been profiled in the *New York Times, Wine Enthusiast* magazine, Salon.com, the *New Orleans Times-Picayune*, and the *Miami Sun-Sentinel*; he's also been featured in the *Washington Post, the Wall Street Journal*, and the *New York Post*. His newest book is *Potions of the Caribbean*.

I not only enjoy drinking tropical cocktails, I also enjoy watching them. And if you waste as much time as I do in front of the TV, eventually you encounter a surprising number of movies in which exotic drinks and/or tiki culture play supporting roles.

1. Pagan Island

1961, directed by Barry Mahon. With Eddie Dew, Nani Maka, Trine Hovelsrud, Sharon Michael, Allison Louise Downe, Bud Irwin

A seaman, stranded on a tropical isle inhabited by women who have never seen a man, angers Queen Kealoha by teaching nubile Nani Maka how to kiss. Turns out Nani's been promised to the Sea God, a jaw-droppingly strange stone statue with a head shaped like two 1950s Cadillac tailfins joined at the nose, and teeth the size of elephant tusks. Miami-based sculptor Lewis Van Dercar created the Sea God; whatever contraband he was ingesting at the time, I want some.

2. The Blue Gardenia

1953, directed by Fritz Lang. With Anne Baxter, Richard Conte, Ann Sothern, Raymond Burr, George Reeves

As Nat King Cole croons the title song, Harry (Burr) seduces Norah (Baxter) in the Coral Room of the Blue Gardenia Supper Club by plying her with tropical drinks—served complete with ice cones and mint sprigs. Harry asks Norah, "Ever see a Polynesian Pearl Diver before?" Norah: "Not served as a drink." Harry: "These aren't really drinks. They're trade winds across cool lagoons. They're the Southern Cross above coral reefs. They're a lovely maiden bathing at the foot of a waterfall." This being a Fritz Lang film, she quaffs one too many of the "South Sea pile drivers" and wakes up the next morning as the prime suspect in Harry's murder.

3. The Frightened City

1961, directed by John Lemont. With Herbert Lom, John Gregson, Sean Connery, Alfred Marks, Yvonne Romain

London's "Taboo Club" features tiki-shaped cocktail menus, scorpion bowls with long straws, and a stiff-upper-lip customer actually dropping his monocle at the sight of hula girls in grass skirts. Connery plays a gangster who's hot for the one bit of crumpet in the floor show who could use a few more pounds, not to mention a few more acting lessons.

4. Donovan's Reef

1963, directed by John Ford. With John Wayne, Lee Marvin, Jack Warden, Elizabeth Allen, Cesar Romero, Dorothy Lamour

Aside from the not inconsiderable pleasures of watching Lee Marvin punch out John Wayne in a tropical island bar, there's the bar itself—which features two tikis guarding the entrance, and another hiding behind the piano (a wise decision, as just about everything in the bar is destroyed except him).

5. Blue Hawaii

1961, directed by Norman Taurog. With Elvis Presley, Joan Blackman, Angela Lansbury, Nancy Walters, Roland Winters, Jenny Maxwell, Pamela Austin, Darlene Tompkins, Christian Kay

Elvis clashes with his wealthy parents when he forsakes them for a grass shack on the beach. It's a nice beach, but I would have stayed with Mom and Dad, who mix impressively authentic-looking mai tais in their swingin' Japanese moderne house.

Though Angela Lansbury played Elvis's mom in *Blue Hawaii*, in real life she was only ten years older than him.

6. How to Stuff a Wild Bikini

1965, directed by William Asher. With Annette Funicello, Dwayne Hickman, Brian Donlevy, Harvey Lembeck, Buster Keaton, Beverly Adams, Mickey Rooney, Frankie Avalon

The title sequence boasts acid-trip animation by "Gumby" creator Art Clokey, in which a gourd briefly morphs into an Easter Island moai. It's all downhill from there, but stick around for the opening scene—featuring Buster Keaton as Bwana, the witch doctor of Goona Goona island, drinking "torpedo juice."

7. Back to the Beach

1987, directed by Lyndall Hobbs. With Frankie Avalon, Annette Funicello, Lori Loughlin, Connie Stevens, Demian Slade

This parody of the 1960s American International "beach party" movies manages to look even more slapdash than the originals. It does round up some original cast members (what the hell *else* did they have to do?), but most of them have not aged well—except for Connie Stevens, who's never looked better, especially with a vintage tiki mug in her hand. And then there's the Big Kahuna Bar, where Frankie Avalon chugs a drink called the "Stunned Mollusk." Cameos include Fishbone, Bob Denver, Alan Hale Jr., Edd Byrnes, Jerry Mathers, Tony Dow, Barbara Billingsley, Dick Dale, Stevie Ray Vaughan, O. J. Simpson, and Pee-wee Herman.

8. Bone

1972, directed by Larry Cohen. With Yaphet Kotto, Andrew Duggan, Joyce Van Patten, Jeannie Berlin, Casey King

Suburban housewife Van Patten offers intruder Kotto a "Wahine's Downfall," which he dismisses as "diabetes on the rocks." Later, repelling her drunken advances, he advises her to "Make yourself another one of them Polynesian drinks, maybe it'll cool you off." I still can't figure out what his problem is, since a rich, sexually frustrated married woman who makes tropical drinks is my idea of a dream date.

9. The Man with Two Brains

1983, directed by Carl Reiner. With Steve Martin, David Warner, Kathleen Turner, Sissy Spacek, George Furth, Peter Hobbs, Earl Boen

In his lab, Dr. Necessitor (Warner) offers his guest Dr. Hfuhruhurr (Martin) a drink: "What would you like?" Hfuhruhurr: "A Tahitian Lady." Necessitor: "Flaming?" Hfuhruhurr: "Oh no, that's strictly for tourists."

10. O. C. and Stiggs

1987, directed by Robert Altman. With Daniel H. Jenkins, Neill Barry, Paul Dooley, Jane Curtin, Martin Mull, Dennis Hopper, Ray Walston, Melvin Van Peebles, Cynthia Nixon, Jon Cryer, King Sunny Adé

In his backyard, which he calls "Tahiti," Martin Mull serves "brown liquor" in Trader Vic skull mugs; set decoration includes Trader Vic table lamps, palm-carved tikis, and lots of vintage rattan furniture. Mull lives next door to the titular teen-aged cutups, who originated in the pages of *National Lampoon* magazine.

11. Tapeheads

1988, directed by Bill Fishman. With John Cusack, Tim Robbins, Mary Crosby, Clu Gulager, Doug McClure, Katy Boyer, Jessica Walter

If you're into '80s nostalgia, then you obviously didn't live through them—and you might be amused by this LA music-biz satire, which features a scene in Kelbo's Polynesian restaurant, "home of the habit-forming spareribs."

Dr. Hfuhruhurr (Steve Martin) and Dr. Necessitor (David Warner) enjoy tropical libations in *The Man with Two Brains*.

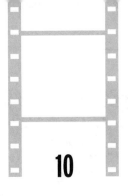

10

Fires, Floods, Crashes, Viruses
Ten Disaster Movies

I n her 1965 essay "The Imagination of Disaster," Susan Sontag offers a theory to explain why movie audiences love to watch things blow up. "To this day, there is nothing like the thrill of watching all those expensive sets come tumbling down," she writes. "In the films it is by means of images and sounds, not words that have to be translated by the imagination, that one can participate in the fantasy of living through one's own death and more, the death of cities, the destruction of humanity itself." Whatever the reason, a good (or very bad) disaster movie can satisfy like nothing else. And sometimes even move you to tears.

1. The Towering Inferno

1974, directed by John Guillermin. With Paul Newman, Steve McQueen, Faye Dunaway, Fred Astaire, Richard Chamberlain, William Holden, Jennifer Jones, O. J. Simpson

We may as well start with a movie that epitomizes the disaster movie. Despite the setup (the opening night gala at the world's tallest skyscraper, which is in San Francisco!), an earthquake does not figure into Irwin Allen's loud and expensive epic. Instead, an all-star cast goes up in flames, courtesy some truly mind-boggling plot contrivances. (Note to building management staff: storing oily rags, fuel

Faye Dunaway and Paul Newman under two tons of greasepaint in *The Towering Inferno.*

containers, and aerosol cans in an out-of-the-way supply closet is a bad idea.) Dated '70s fashions and furnishings, some terrible dialogue, and widescreen vistas of tons of stuff on fire are all part of the fun.

2. Crack in the World

1965, directed by Andrew Marton. With Dana Andrews, Janette Scott, Kieron Moore, Alexander Knox

Disaster '60s style. Exploding a nuclear device deep underground sounds like the perfect way to tap into the earth's geothermal energy, right? No, not exactly; but if you're looking for the perfect way to split the planet in half, you might be on the right track. This somewhat forgotten yarn is compact and entertaining, with some cool work by French special effects wiz Eugène Lourié.

3. A Night to Remember

1958, directed by Roy Ward Baker. With Kenneth More, Ronald Allen, Robert Ayres, Honor Blackman

Several decades before James Cameron's blockbuster, director Baker and screenwriter Eric Ambler drew on original sources to tell the story of the sinking of the *Titanic.* It's refreshingly straightforward, keeping the melodrama to a minimum and sticking instead to a strict chronology of events. The special effects are modest but effective. Look fast for an unbilled Sean Connery playing a crewman.

4. The Hurricane

1937, directed by John Ford. With Dorothy Lamour, Jon Hall, Mary Astor, C. Aubrey Smith, Thomas Mitchell, Raymond Massey

John Ford didn't make just Westerns. This bit of exotic hokum centers on a motley group of expatriates and natives in the South Seas, their loves and lusts, climaxing with (you guessed it) a gigantic tropical storm. Glistening cinematography by Bert Glennon makes everything look improbably glamorous, which is one of the movie's chief pleasures. The 1979 remake, which starred Mia Farrow and Jason Robards, boasts the tagline "There is only one safe place . . . in each other's arms."

5. Night of the Comet

1984, directed by Thom Eberhardt. With Catherine Mary Stewart, Kelli Maroney, Robert Beltran, Mary Woronov

A passing comet reduces everyone on the planet to dust, with the apparent exceptions being valley girl Reggie and her 16-year old sister, Sam. They wander through a deserted LA looking for fellow survivors. This cult favorite is a zesty blend of social satire, zombie horror, sci-fi, and romance. A nonstop soundtrack of ersatz '80s pop (a Top 40 radio station figures prominently in the story) is a nice touch.

6. The Exterminating Angel

1962, directed by Luis Buñuel. With Silvia Pinal, Enrique Rambal, Claudio Brook, José Baviera, Augusto Benedico, Lucy Gallardo

After an elegant dinner party, the moneyed hosts and their guests retire to the drawing room for music and cigars. But at the end of the evening they find themselves unable to leave the room, imprisoned by some mysterious force of social etiquette. After being trapped for several days they begin to starve and are soon reduced to living like animals. Master surrealist Buñuel takes the conventions of the disaster movie and fashions them into a fable about the stupidity of the wealthy. It's funny and frightening at the same time, with an especially pointed finale.

7. The Andromeda Strain

1971, directed by Robert Wise. With Arthur Hill, James Olson, Kate Reid, David Wayne, Paula Kelly

Based on a novel by Michael Crichton, this sober sci-fi thriller about the race to neutralize an alien virus is noteworthy for a striking electronic score by Gil Mellé and nifty special effects, courtesy Douglas Trumbull (*2001: A Space Odyssey*). Its scale, especially for a disaster movie, is rather intimate, focusing on a small town in New

Mexico and a futuristic science lab. The 2008 miniseries, starring Benjamin Bratt, doesn't stick as closely to Crichton's novel.

8. Stalker

1979, directed by Andrei Tarkovsky. With Aleksandr Kaidanovsky. Alisa Frejndlikh, Anatoli Solonitsyn, Nikolai Grinko, Natasha Abramova

At the center of a mysterious industrial wasteland known as the Zone lies a room where one's deepest wish comes true. Many have made the journey and never returned. Now, with the help of a psychic guide known as a stalker, two adventurers try their luck. Tarkovsky's eerie, cerebral tale is slow paced but hypnotic, once you adjust. Partially shot at an abandoned chemical factory in Estonia, it's filled with stunning imagery and the most intricate sound design this side of David Lynch's *Eraserhead.*

9. Fearless

1993, directed by Peter Weir. With Jeff Bridges, Isabella Rossellini, Rosie Perez, Tom Hulce, John Turturro

After surviving a horrific plain crash, Max Klein (Bridges) undergoes a huge personality shift, somehow convinced that he's now invulnerable. As his wife and doctor try to understand what's happened to him, Max finds himself drawn to a fellow survivor (Perez) whose life is falling apart. Sharply drawn character work from all concerned is aided and abetted by one of the most visceral, harrowing depictions of a plane crash ever put on film. Also notable is the movie's breathtaking use of Górecki's Symphony no. 3.

10. Trouble the Water

2008, directed by Tia Lessen and Carl Deal

The week before Hurricane Katrina made landfall, New Orleans resident Kimberly Roberts bought a camcorder off the street for $20 and began to record moments of daily life in the Lower Ninth Ward. When the storm hit and power was cut, she kept filming until the battery ran out, documenting how she, her husband, Scott, and their neighbors fought for survival: relocating to an attic, punching holes in the roof, and using a boat and even a surfboard that happened to be floating by as means of escape. This documentary interweaves Roberts's footage with clips of news coverage to powerful effect; the contrast between the pontification of the slickers on TV and the life-or-death struggle of the refugees is fascinating.

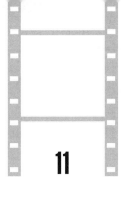

11

Flops That Actually
Aren't Half Bad

More than ever before, filmmaking exists at the mercy of the bottom line. In the world of big-budget filmmaking, most investors will sink money only into a movie they expect will earn them a healthy return. And the more a movie costs to produce, the higher the expectations. Movies fail at the box office for many reasons. Some flops, perhaps even the majority, are just plain terrible. But there are many that flop because of other factors: they're ahead of their time, they're promoted badly (or not at all), or the original audience just doesn't get them. Though the box office can be cruel, time can be kind. Here are some that, with the benefit of hindsight, deserve another look.

1. Citizen Kane

1941, directed by Orson Welles. With Orson Welles, Joseph Cotten, Dorothy Comingore, Everett Sloane, Ray Collins, George Coulouris, Agnes Moorehead, Paul Stewart, Ruth Warrick

Its storytelling structure, involving multiple flashbacks; Gregg Toland's deep-focus cinematography, allowing the entire frame to come to life; its canny use of symbolism to illustrate the characters' psychology; Bernard Herrmann's eerie, evocative music score; its use of special effects, seamlessly integrated into the fabric of the movie: nearly every innovative technique in *Citizen Kane* is still in use today. (If you don't believe me, try watching it on a double feature with *The Social Network* and note the stunning resemblance.) But media mogul William Randolph Hearst, who thought *Citizen Kane* a thinly veiled portrait of himself, did everything in his power to blackball it, and audience reaction was lukewarm. It's now widely considered the greatest film ever made—go figure.

2. It's a Wonderful Life

1946, directed by Frank Capra. With James Stewart, Donna Reed, Lionel Barrymore, Henry Travers, Thomas Mitchell, Gloria Grahame, H. B. Warner

The most beloved Christmas movie of all time was a disappointment at the box office during its initial release, and scattered among the positive reviews were others like this one from Bosley Crowther at the *New York Times:* "The weakness of this picture, from this reviewer's point of view, is the sentimentality of it—its illusory concept of life. Mr. Capra's nice people are charming, his small town is a quite beguiling place and his pattern for solving problems is most optimistic and facile." And a Happy New Year to you, too, Mr. Crowther—in jail!

3. Bringing Up Baby

1938, directed by Howard Hawks. With Katharine Hepburn, Cary Grant, Charles Ruggles, Walter Catlett, May Robson, Fritz Feld, Barry Fitzgerald

Getting the drift yet? The American Film Institute named it one of the one hundred greatest American films of all time, but *Bringing Up Baby* barely broke even when it was first released. It's an all-time screwball comedy classic. Grant plays a prissy bespectacled paleontologist who gets mixed up with Susan, a hare-brained heiress (Hepburn). Somehow Baby, a leopard that Susan's brother has entrusted to her for safekeeping, figures into the whole thing, too, naturally leading to a missing dinosaur bone, wild chases, and a night in jail. Hawks keeps things moving at a frantic pace that's exhilarating.

4. Cleopatra

1963, directed by Joseph L. Mankiewicz. With Elizabeth Taylor, Richard Burton, Rex Harrison, Roddy McDowall, Martin Landau, Hume Cronyn, George Cole

A different kind of example. This notorious boondoggle was 1963's *highest-grossing* film, yet still took years to make back its $44 million production cost—which, adjusted for inflation, still makes it the most expensive film ever made. Guess what? It's actually not bad. (At just over four hours long, you certainly get

Elizabeth Taylor was reportedly paid $7 million to star in *Cleopatra*, which included sixty-five costume changes for Taylor alone.

your money's worth.) Cleopatra's entrance into Rome, an absurdly lavish procession bursting with extravagance, remains unmatched for sheer screen splendor. The making of the film might have been a nightmare but the performances are surprisingly solid, especially McDowall as the wily Octavian.

5. Secret Ceremony

1968, directed by Joseph Losey. With Elizabeth Taylor, Mia Farrow, Robert Mitchum, Peggy Ashcroft, Pamela Brown

Yes indeed, there's no doubt that Liz had her share of duds. Here she's a whore who meets childlike Farrow by chance one day on a bus. Taylor resembles Farrow's dead mother, and Farrow resembles Taylor's dead daughter. They move in together and begin a twisted game of role playing that grows increasingly ominous. Throw into the mix creepy child molester Mitchum, and you've got one really really bizarre film, which (understandably) baffled audiences when it was initially released. Seen today it's actually not as campy as it sounds, thanks to director Losey's poker-faced handling of the far-out story and remarkably believable performances by all. Taylor even gets to show off some mod '60s fashions by Christian Dior. Farrow starred in *Rosemary's Baby* the same year; what a double feature!

6. The Adventures of Baron Munchausen

1989, directed by Terry Gilliam. With John Neville, Sarah Polley, Eric Idle, Jonathan Pryce, Robin Williams, Oliver Reed, Uma Thurman

> "Reality? Your reality, sir, is lies and balderdash, and I'm delighted to say that I have no grasp of it whatsoever."
>
> —BARON MUNCHAUSEN, *THE ADVENTURES OF BARON MUNCHAUSEN*

A combination of alleged cost overruns and a studio that turned its back on the finished movie doomed this sumptuously filmed fantasy about the exploits of the world's greatest liar. But what ended up on-screen is pure delight. In the late eighteenth century, with their city under siege by the Turkish army, the regal Baron regales a young girl (Polley) with tales of his various adventures, soon hatching a plan to escape the city in a giant balloon. Their subsequent voyages include a trip to outer space, with Williams in a hilarious turn as the King of the Moon, possessing a detachable head that floats around at will. Monty Python's Gilliam and Idle endow the movie with puckish wit that complements the movie's outlandish elements.

7. Playtime

1967, directed by Jacques Tati. With Jacques Tati, Barbara Dennek, Jacqueline Lecomte, Valérie Camille, France Rumilly, Luce Bonifassy, Marc Monjou, Yves Barsacq, Billy Kearns

Tati spent three years and enormous sums of money to create this extraordinary film, a nearly wordless comedy featuring Tati's beloved character M. Hulot. In a series of loosely wound setpieces, Hulot makes his way through a labyrinthine, ultramodern Paris (a recurring joke features the Eiffel Tower reflected in various windows). Although critically successful, audiences found it out of step with France's "new" cinema, films like *Belle de jour* and *Week End*. It flopped, and Tati eventually declared bankruptcy. Now beautifully restored, it's the perfect movie to watch on a giant screen, stuffed with complicated sight gags unfurling in every part of the frame.

8. The Intruder

1962, directed by Roger Corman. With William Shatner, Frank Maxwell, Beverly Lunsford, Robert Emhardt, Leo Gordon, Charles Barnes, Charles Beaumont, Katherine Smith

In the title role, Shatner offers an eye-opening performance as Adam Cramer, member of a shadowy organization called the Patrick Henry Society. He arrives in the small Southern hamlet of Caxton to stir up racial hatred, inciting the whites in the town to fight the impending integration of a local school. Unflinching in its depictions of mob violence, including a cross burning and a church bombing, it makes 1967's more celebrated *In the Heat of the Night* seem tame by comparison. It was filmed on a shoestring by B-movie king Corman, who once remarked, "This was the first film of mine that ever lost money . . . but it didn't lose too much money."

Though the film was a flop at the box office, the ultramodern world of Jacques Tati's *Playtime* laid the groundwork for later movies like *Brazil*.

9. One from the Heart

1982, directed by Francis (Ford) Coppola. With Teri Garr, Frederic Forrest, Raul Julia, Nastassia Kinski, Harry Dean Stanton, Lainie Kazan

This deeply peculiar movie answers the question "What would it be like if Howard Hawks and Fellini had codirected *Moulin Rouge!* instead of Baz Luhrmann?" Long-time sweethearts Franny (Garr) and Hank (Forrest) break up and have romantic escapades with other people, she with a sensitive lounge pianist (Julia) and he with an exotic circus dancer (Kinski). And it's all set to an almost continuous song score by Tom Waits and Crystal Gayle. This neon musical fable, set in Las Vegas but shot entirely on soundstages, sunk like a stone the moment it was released, hastening the bankruptcy of Coppola's American Zoetrope Studios. But its sheer audacity is arresting, with several bravura moments that (almost) convince you Coppola pulled off one of the most personal films to ever emerge from 1980s Hollywood.

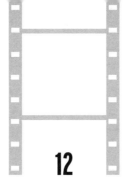

12

That Magic Moment
Homoerotic Display in Heteronormative Cinema
By David Kodeski

David Kodeski is the creator of *David Kodeski's True Life Tales,* an ongoing series of critically acclaimed solo performances. His *Niagara! (You Should Have Been Yosemite)* inspired a Niagara-based episode of National Public Radio's *This American Life.* A radio version of *Another Lousy Day* was produced by Long Haul Productions and was heard on *All Things Considered.*

Rob's note > Remember when I commented earlier on the movies' unparalleled capacity for subtext? Here, David Kodeski excavates subterranean desires lurking in six vintage flicks.

1. Love Has Many Faces

1965, directed by Alexander Singer. With Lana Turner, Cliff Robertson, Hugh O'Brian, Ron Husmann, Ruth Roman, Virginia Grey

The sunny beaches of mid-1960s Acapulco are filled with suntanned rent boys and the mature, lonely, and very wealthy ladies who help keep them in designer bathing suits. Early on in this Lana Turner costume change cavalcade, Ruth Roman and Virginia Grey are spotted by a pair of gigolos played by Hugh O'Brian and Ron Husmann. As they cross the sands, O'Brian, in a canary yellow bikini, pauses for a moment to show off his muscled prowess by suspending himself horizontally on a pole situated amid the palm trees. It is an impressive display of hirsute musculature, and the Ruth Roman character is suitably impressed. Acrobatics concluded,

O'Brian and Husmann continue toward the women and are questioned along the way by a detective. A fellow gigolo has recently washed up on one of the pristine beaches, and the dick is looking for answers. O'Brian is cocky and self-assured as he brushes off the law, his masculinity fully on display beneath the thin fabric of his swimsuit, leading his way like a diving rod across the hot white sands.

2. Picnic

1955, directed by Joshua Logan. With William Holden, Kim Novak, Rosalind Russell, Betty Field, Cliff Robertson

Under the opening credits William Holden, stripped to the waist, washes himself in the rushing waters of an overflow dam. Lamentably, his torso is mostly obscured by the credits. Lucky for us, a few minutes into the film, he's led by a kindly old woman to a trash barrel situated behind a shed where he's to burn some trash in exchange for the food she's just given him. Holden quickly removes his brown jacket and denim shirt. Apparently unmoved by his pulchritude, the woman throws in a match and wishes him well. The flames in the barrel begin to rise, and Holden grabs a long wooden stick, jamming it into the conflagration. Across the way and through some trees, Rosalind Russell wanders through her yard, her face slathered in cold cream, her hair in curlers. She notices this hot, shirtless, and sweaty stranger. She recognizes what we recognize but is unable to give in to her more sinister urges and does the only thing she can do—which is to flee. Moments

William Holden goes shirtless in *Picnic*. A few years later he also stripped down for *The Bridge on the River Kwai*.

later Holden rescues Kim Novak from the attentions of a pesky paramour and she goes to thank him. Between them the barrel of trash roars, and Novak kittenishly brushes out her ponytail. She's obviously smitten and clutches a long, thick, fence-post, caressing it before running off through the bushes, toward the safety of home. But, before entering the house, she takes one last lingering look at Holden's sweaty magnificence. It is a shame that director Joshua Logan does not allow us to do the same.

3. Back Street

1961, directed by David Miller. With Susan Hayward, John Gavin, Vera Miles, Virginia Grey

Ostensibly just outside Rome, but more realistically just down the way from Holly-wood's Universal Studios lot, 43-year-old Susan Hayward and 30-year-old John Gavin run from the sea and throw themselves down onto their ready beach towel. Invigorated and energized by their "Mediterranean" dip, they discuss their three-day beach house extramarital idyll. Gavin is Paul Saxon, department store mogul, and is unfortunately married to a shrewishly alcoholic Vera Miles; Hayward is Miss Rae Smith, internationally renowned fashion designer who has given up her virtue to Gavin in the film's turgid first act. After meeting and parting in Nebraska, then meeting and parting in New York, they are at last together again in Rome, and as they discuss the what-ifs of their lives, Gavin rests on his back, his flat belly still heaving with exertion, his chest still wet (studio oiled), draped with Hayward's arms and roving hand. And it is this roving hand that dominates this minute-long scene. Perfectly manicured, its nails painted a glossy nude, the hand glides over Gavin's left pectoral, insistently plucking at his chest hairs, sliding up, and circling around. It seems disembodied, to have a mind of its own, and determined to distract the viewer from the overwritten dialogue of its owner. It is here that the hand and the viewer become one.

4. The Driver's Seat

1974, directed by Giuseppe Patroni Griffi. With Elizabeth Taylor, Ian Bannen, Guido Mannari

As Susan Hayward demonstrated in *Back Street,* it's all in the wrist. In *The Driver's Seat,* there's a certain verisimilitude to the way the garage mechanic Guido Mannari reaches into the depths of his white coveralls and adjusts his erection before telling Elizabeth Taylor, "The front seat falls back. So, make yourself comfortable." It is a tour de force of hand acting and may have something to do with the way he separates his index and middle fingers and curves his thumb toward his palm as he pulls his hand out of the obviously humid darkness. In a later scene we see how Taylor and Mannari ended up in the white car at the end of a "shortcut" on the way to the Rome Hilton. There's been a terrorist bombing in the streets, and Taylor has fled to Mannari's auto repair garage. Once there, she fairly seduces him as he attempts to clean a grease stain from the loud pattern of her coat. Based on the Muriel Sparks novella, this unjustly maligned movie is slyly over the top with a terrific performance by Taylor and great supporting players like Mannari's hand. The rest of him isn't so bad either.

5. Clash by Night

1952, directed by Fritz Lang. With Barbara Stanwyck, Robert Ryan, Paul Douglas, Marilyn Monroe, Keith Andes

It's quite an exciting moment when Barbara Stanwyck, pressed up against the kitchen sink, shoves her hand up Robert Ryan's wifebeater. It's a climactic moment in one of the more kitchen sink-y of pot boiling kitchen sink dramas and easily matches the overwrought dialogue by Clifford Odets. Ryan's back becomes a study in deltoid, rhomboid, and supraspinatus rippling as Stanwyck succumbs to her pent-up passions. Director Lang then cuts to a shot of the statue of Father Serra overlooking Monterey Bay—shot from the back, of course. It's a fine visual joke, and the next shot brings us to a boat deck in the bay where Stanwyck's now cuck-olded husband, played by Paul Douglas, mends nets with a shirtless Keith Andes.

6. The Bullfighter and the Lady

1951, directed by Budd Boetticher. With Robert Stack, Gilbert Roland, Katy Jurado, Joy Page

One might think that the hottest moment in a movie featuring an amazingly fit, trim, and blond Robert Stack as a wannabe matador would take place in the steam room where he meets Gilbert Roland to discusses the possibility of becoming a real *torero.* You might also think it occurs as Stack, crossing the *ruedo* improperly dressed but obviously (even from the nosebleed seats of the bull ring) dressing left. Instead, it is Stack's closeups that convey the white-hot heat burning within him. Following a scene in which Katy Jurado dresses down a *borracho* who has insulted her matador husband Gilbert Roland, Stack and his love interest, Joy Page, discuss the incident. Intended as a 124-minute film, *The Bullfighter and the Lady* was cut down on its release to 87 minutes so that it could fit on a double bill. Restored by the UCLA Film and Television Archive, some of the restored footage appears slightly over exposed, including certain shots of this scene. In these close-ups, as Stack urges Page to "go someplace we can talk," his features and his white-blond hair appear as though they might combust at any second.

13

Man ♥ Sheep, Teen ♥ 1958 Plymouth Fury,
and Seven Other Unusual Romances

No chick flicks on this list! Instead, think of romances that resemble this quote from *The Naked Gun: From the Files of Police Squad!:* "It's the same old story. Boy finds girl, boy loses girl, girl finds boy, boy forgets girl, boy remembers girl, girls dies in a tragic blimp accident over the Orange Bowl on New Year's Day."

1. Murderous Bull Terrier ♥ Master in *Baxter*

1989, directed by Jérôme Boivin. With Jean Mercure, Lise Delamare, Jacques Spiesser, Catherine Ferran

In voiceover, an intelligent dog relates the story of his quest for the perfect owner. It certainly isn't the old lady who receives Baxter as a gift (he trips her in an attempt to cause a fatal fall) or the young married couple who takes him in next (he doesn't approve of their baby, and tries to kill it). Could it be his next master, a boy in the neighborhood with budding sociopathic tendencies who admires Hitler? This blacker-than-black comedy was featured as an episode of John Waters's TV series *Movies That Will Corrupt You.*

2. Artist ♥ Writer in *Carrington*

1995, directed by Christopher Hampton. With Emma Thompson, Jonathan Pryce, Steven Waddington, Rufus Sewell

This historical drama details the frustrating lifelong relationship between Dora Carrington, a gifted painter, and Lytton Strachey, a gay author. Although clearly in love, they can never quite bring themselves to commit to each other. Their story unfolds between 1915 and 1932 against the vivid intellectual backdrop of the Bloomsbury Group. Thompson and Pryce have never been better. Hampton, who also scripted, was awarded a Special Jury Prize at the Cannes Film Festival.

3. Personal Computer ♥ Girl in *Electric Dreams*

1984, directed by Steve Barron. With Lenny von Dohlen, Virginia Madsen, Maxwell Caulfield, Bud Cort

What a time capsule: at first a personal computer named Edgar plays Cyrano to help nerdy Miles score with the attractive girl upstairs, then decides that "he" wants her for himself! It's a story crying out for an update (perhaps involving an iPad app?), although Oscar-nominee Madsen probably wishes this movie could vanish from her filmography. It's only fitting that the score is by electronic pop pioneer Giorgio Moroder, who has a cameo as a radio station executive.

4. Monk ♥ Temple in *Mishima: A Life in Four Chapters*

1985, directed by Paul Schrader. With Ken Ogata, Masayuki Shionoya, Hiroshi Mikami, Junya Fukuda, Shigeto Tachihara

This unique biography of the controversial and influential Japanese writer Yukio Mishima alternates snippets of his life (in black and white) with stripped-down adaptations of some of his stories (shown in color). One of them is his novel *Temple of the Golden Pavilion,* which concerns a novice monk's devotion to and eventual obsession with the temple he serves. Stunning cinematography by John Bailey and music by Philip Glass make this film a feast for the senses.

5. Teen ♥ 1958 Plymouth Fury in *Christine*

1983, directed by John Carpenter. With Keith Gordon, John Stockwell, Alexandra Paul, Harry Dean Stanton

A teenager becomes a bit obsessed with the beat-up vintage car he's been restoring to its former glory. When the source material is a Stephen King novel, the odds are pretty good that said automobile is possessed by an evil spirit, which caused the demise of its previous owner. *The Love Bug* it ain't. As with most of his other films, Carpenter also contributed the movie's soundtrack. Keith Gordon is frighteningly intense as Arnie Cunningham, the shy teenage car enthusiast who eventually goes off the deep end.

> "You better watch what you say about my car. She's real sensitive."
>
> —ARNIE CUNNINGHAM, *CHRISTINE*

6. Astoundingly Neurotic Man ♥ Woman in *Modern Romance*

1981, directed by Albert Brooks. With Albert Brooks, Kathryn Harrold, Bruno Kirby, James L. Brooks, George Kennedy

The story goes that shortly after *Modern Romance* came out, Brooks got a random phone call late one night from Stanley Kubrick, who said, "That's the picture I've been trying to make for the last twenty years. How the hell did you do it?" Every time Robert gets back together with Mary, they decide it would be better to break up; yet when they're apart Robert goes crazy imagining what Mary might be doing without him, triggering yet another reconciliation. The ultimate cringe-inducing comedy, it's a must for fans of *Curb Your Enthusiasm*.

7. Playwright ♥ Portrait in *Somewhere in Time*

1980, directed by Jeannot Szwarc. With Christopher Reeve, Jane Seymour, Christopher Plummer, Teresa Wright

Richard Matheson adapts his own novel, *Bid Time Return*. A man falls in love with the beautiful woman depicted in a painting at the vintage hotel where he's staying and uses self-hypnosis to journey back in time to meet her. Although somewhat ignored when released, this romance has aged well, with excellent use of location filming on Mackinac Island in Michigan. Reeve and Seymour make a dreamy couple, and John Barry's lush score, which incorporates Rachmaninoff, is also a big asset.

8. Sci-fi Fans ♥ Star Trek in *Trekkies*

1997, directed by Roger Nygard. With Denise Crosby, Frank D'Amico, Barbara Adams

Not just for those who have already been initiated, this entertaining documentary profiles diehard American fans of the various *Star Trek* incarnations, from the original '60s TV show to its feature films and *Next Generation* spin-off (which was on the air when this movie came out). Many original cast members are on hand to comment on the phenomenon. Refreshingly, Nygard doesn't make fun of these devotees even as he documents their eccentricities (such as wearing phasers to the office,

Denise Crosby, who played Security Chief Tasha Yar on *Star Trek: The Next Generation*, hosts *Trekkies*, a quintessential look at the series' phenomenon.

speaking in Klingon, and dressing up in Starfleet unforms). A 2007 sequel, *Trekkies 2,* expands its reach to the rest of the globe.

9. Man ♥ Sheep in *Everything You Always Wanted to Know about Sex* (*But Were Afraid to Ask)*

1972, directed by Woody Allen. With Gene Wilder, Tony Randall, Burt Reynolds, Louise Lasser, John Carradine, Woody Allen

Allen's movie consists of various sketches riffing on mankind's sexual foibles. The episodes are highly variable in quality (although the segment about the rampaging breast does have its defenders), but a standout is most definitely Gene Wilder's vignette. He plays mild-mannered Dr. Ross, who finds himself falling for one of his patients—a shapely sheep named Daisy. Their pillow talk is hilarious.

14

Eight Films about Doomed Romance

By Eugenia Williamson

Eugenia Williamson is a staff writer for *The Boston Phoenix*
and an associate editor at *The Baffler* magazine. A native
of Chicago and former circulation manager of the Newberry
Library, she currently lives in Somerville, Massachusetts. She
has watched *Sid and Nancy* at least fifty times.

I've suffered through my fair share of failed relationships, but none thus far have involved anything more dramatic than a slammed door and a few swears. Not so for the following movies. All films—even *C.H.U.D.*—contain an element of doomed romance, but very few capture the exquisite torture of a broken heart; here is a list of ones that do.

1. Jules and Jim

1962, directed by Francois Truffaut. With Jeanne Moreau, Oskar Werner, Henri Serre

Jeanne Moreau's Catherine, a prim femme fatale, vacillates between best friends Jules (Werner) and Jim (Serre). Never was there a love triangle so tortured, or so wholesome—had any errant preschoolers stumbled onto the set during the climactic scene when Catherine primly sings "Le Tourbillon" to her awestruck paramours, they surely would have been charmed. Not so for the film's climax when, after an unseemly number of switch-offs, the trio drives off a verdant cliff.

2. Human Nature

2001, directed by Michel Gondry. With Tim Robbins, Patricia Arquette, Rhys Ifans, Rosie Perez, Miranda Otto, Peter Dinklage, Mary Kay Place, Robert Forster, Hilary Duff

In addition to exploring the philosophical underpinnings of civilization, Charlie Kaufman's criminally underrated follow-up to *Being John Malkovich* explores a simple question: can extremely hairy women find true love? In this farcical meditation, the hirsute Lila (Arquette) meets Dr. Nathan Bronfman (Robbins) after deciding to undergo electrolysis. Together, they capture a feral man from the forest (Ifans), name him Puff, and teach him table manners. When Nathan leaves Lila for his comely and smooth research assistant, Lila springs Puff, and, for a time, the pair live out their days in a forest idyll—until Lila is once against bested by her hairless foe.

3. Sid and Nancy

1986, directed by Alex Cox. With Chloe Webb, Gary Oldman, David Hayman, Debby Bishop, Andrew Schofield, Courtney Love, Xander Berkeley

Half the fun of watching *Sid and Nancy* is derived from watching very skinny people in outlandish clothes get swallowed up by the grayness of '70s London and New York. The other half is watching Chloe Webb and Gary Oldman act their little guts out as a pair of goofy, inordinately maladjusted heroin addicts. The film begins with a moderately embarrassing attempt at capturing the visceral thrill of the Sex Pistols and punk rock in London, circa 1976. But by the time Webb calls her mother to tell her she's married, it has evolved into an insanely bleak meditation on love and death and individualism, a Cold War update of *Bonnie and Clyde*. Speaking of . . .

4. Bonnie and Clyde

1967, directed by Arthur Penn. With Warren Beatty, Faye Dunaway, Michael J. Pollard, Gene Hackman, Estelle Parsons, Denver Pyle, Gene Wilder

In addition to being the best-looking couple ever to appear on film, Faye Dunaway and Warren Beatty as Bonnie Parker and Clyde Barrow have the most tragic story. Imagine being that glamorous *and* celibate! By the time they are taken out in a hail of bullets, it's almost a relief.

5. Henry Fool

1997, directed by Hal Hartley. With Thomas Jay Ryan, James Urbaniak, Parker Posey, Liam Aiken, Maria Porter, James Saito, Kevin Corrigan

Simon (Urbaniak) and Fay Grim (Posey) live in a sad little house with their morbidly depressed mother in a gray, depressing town. Enter Henry Fool (Ryan), a drunk, greasy artiste on the lam, who rents out their basement apartment to complete his magnum opus. Simon and Fay both fall in love with him, in their fashion, but it's Fay whom Henry marries after too much espresso leads to an inadvertent proposal in the can. When tragedy strikes, Henry must skip town again, leaving Fay and their adorable young son to pine for him. *Henry Fool* is a sentimental—never mawkish—tour de force.

6. The Music Lovers

1970, directed by Ken Russell. With Richard Chamberlain, Glenda Jackson, Kenneth Colley, Christopher Gable, Max Adrian, Izabella Telezynska, Maureen Pryor, Andrew Faulds

Even by Ken Russell standards, this film is bonkers. Tchaikovsky (Chamberlain) attempts to deny his homosexuality through his marriage to sex-crazed Nina

Faye Dunaway and Warren Beatty try some target practice in *Bonnie and Clyde*. Although the movie has plenty of violence, this is one love story without any nudity whatsoever.

(Jackson). Whoops! As Tchaikovsky sublimates his desires into genius compositions—depicted in Russell's trademark phantasmagorical style—Nina is driven mad by her husband's ambivalence. Tchaikovsky commits slow suicide via tainted water, Nina ends up in the world's most disturbing mental institution, and Russell gets to film them falling apart.

7. Breaking the Waves

1996, directed by Lars von Trier. With Emily Watson, Stellan Skarsgård, Katrin Cartlidge, Udo Kier

Emily Watson gives the performance of a lifetime as Bess, a simpleton who often talks, out loud, to God. Bess falls head over heels for Jan (Skarsgård), an oily, lecherous oilman. Shortly after their wedding, Jan becomes paralyzed and tells Bess to engage in increasingly humiliating sex acts for his own inert titillation. When Bess is stabbed to death in a gangbang, Jan can, miraculously, walk again.

8. Kicking and Screaming

1995, directed by Noah Baumbach. With Olivia d'Abo, Elliott Gould, Eric Stoltz, Parker Posey, Chris Eigeman, Josh Hamilton, Sam Gould, Catherine Kellner, Jonathan Baumbach

Compared to *Margot at the Wedding, Greenberg,* and *The Squid and the Whale,* Noah Baumbach's directorial debut suffers from a conspicuous absence of wholly unsympathetic characters. Though the chatty recent grads who populate *Kicking and Screaming* aren't careening id monsters of Greenbergian proportions, they're no less compelling to watch. Good-hearted Grover (Hamilton), adrift after girlfriend Jane (d'Abo) takes off on a vision quest to Prague, is too distracted by pop culture references to chase after her. Through flashbacks, we learn of the distinctly collegial origins of their love—a smoky bar, a writing seminar—and can almost smell the self-consciousness of their fumblings. By the time Grover realizes he needs Jane, fate intervenes against love, and they are doomed.

> "Okay, the way I see it, if we were an old couple, dated for years, graduated, away from all these scholastic complications, and I reached over and kissed you, you wouldn't say a word. You'd be delighted. Probably. But if I was to do that now it'd be quite forward, and if I did it the first time we ever met you probably would hit me. . . . I just wish we were an old couple so I could do that."
>
> —GROVER, *KICKING AND SCREAMING*

15

Movies Guaranteed to Make You Cry

New research suggests that crying is a way for the body to flush toxins from its system. And who doesn't need a good cry now and then? Here are some prime specimens that'll open the floodgates before the end credits roll.

1. Steel Magnolias

1989, directed by Herbert Ross. With Shirley MacLaine, Olympia Dukakis, Dolly Parton, Sally Field, Daryl Hannah, Julia Roberts

I'll kick things off with a movie that would certainly be on many people's lists. Robert Harling's play about a Louisiana beauty parlor and its social circle is translated into a cinematic weepie deluxe under the steady hand of director Ross. Unlike the original play, a few men make some token appearances. But really this is all about the ladies, as they hold on to one another through love, heartbreak, happiness, and (spoiler/not really a spoiler) terminal illness.

2. Shadowlands

1993, directed by Sir Richard Attenborough. With Anthony Hopkins, Debra Winger, Peter Firth, Edward Hardwicke, Joseph Mazzello, James Frain, Julian Fellowes

Speaking of terminal illnesses . . . In *Shadowlands,* C. S. Lewis (Hopkins), famous author of *The Chronicles of Narnia,* falls in love for the first time in his life with an

American writer, Joy Gresham (Winger). Their bliss is cut short when she is diagnosed with cancer and slowly begins to die. Winger is perfect as the brash Yank, but it's really the scenes where Hopkins comes to terms with the fact that he's fallen in love that are painfully tender. To see the pain and joy mingle in his rapidly moistening eyes is enough to make anyone lose control of their tear ducts.

3. Dancer in the Dark

2000, directed by Lars von Trier. With Björk, Catherine Deneuve, David Morse, Peter Stormare, Cara Seymour, Siobhan Fallon Hogan, Joel Grey

Clearly there's something about physical ailments on-screen that really get to us. This melodrama about Selma (Björk), a poor factory worker desperate to earn enough money for her son's eyesight-saving operation, comes off at first as an avant-garde musical. Shot in dour tones on digital video, the film breaks into sudden musical interludes captured from odd camera angles. But at heart it's an old-fashioned, expertly manipulative tearjerker, drawing most of its considerable power from Björk's intense performance, a hypnotic mixture of naiveté, wisdom, strength, and vulnerability. Even if you despise the feeling of being manhandled by von Trier's pretentious aesthetics (as I do), you'll be crushed by the story's shattering finale.

John Hurt as John Merrick in *The Elephant Man*. The hood with the single eyehole was David Lynch's idea.

4. Away from Her

2006, directed by Sarah Polley. With Julie Christie, Gordon Pinsent, Olympia Dukakis, Kristen Thomson, Michael Murphy, Grace Lynn Kung, Wendy Crewson

She places the skillet in the freezer. She knows she's done something odd, but she can't remember *why* it's odd. Christie gives a spellbinding performance as Fiona, a woman coming to grips with the onset of Alzheimer's. Determined to plan for her future while she's still capable of making her own choices, she insists that her devoted husband admit her to an attended care facility. His devastation is compounded when she no longer remembers him and becomes attached to another resident. This heartrending story plays out against beautiful scenery of the Ontario countryside, infused with moments of

> "You know what I'd like? I'd like to make love, and then I'd like you to go. Because I need to stay here and if you make it hard for me, I might cry so hard I'll never stop."
>
> –FIONA ANDERSON, *AWAY FROM HER*

great wisdom and tenderness. The entire cast is excellent, especially Dukakis as a feisty senior who refuses to settle down into a quiet life.

5. Dumbo

1941, animation supervised by Ben Sharpsteen

Preoccupied with *Fantasia,* Walt Disney rushed *Dumbo* through production in order to get a feature into theaters quickly. The simple story of a baby elephant who comes to accept his enormous ears, it's only sixty-four minutes long but packed with unforgettable moments: "Look Out for Mr. Stork," the unloading of the circus train during a rainstorm, and especially "Pink Elephants on Parade," as delightful a sequence as any from cinema's golden age. But "Baby Mine" is what'll put the lump in your throat. Mrs. Jumbo straining her trunk to reach out of that cage, just enough to cradle Dumbo and swing him gently back and forth . . .

6. The Elephant Man

1980, directed by David Lynch. With John Hurt, Anthony Hopkins, Anne Bancroft, Freddie Jones

Two films about elephants on my list? What's up with that? Well, I'm no psycho-analyst, but both *Dumbo* and *The Elephant Man* speak very powerfully about what it is to be a freak and an outcast. In an Oscar-nominated performance, Hurt plays John Merrick, a horribly deformed man in Victorian England who is given a modicum of dignity for the first time in life thanks to the interventions of a respected surgeon (Hopkins). I really can't think of a film in this genre that's more moving. Lynch and master cinematographer Freddie Francis create a world rich with period texture. The ending is a heartbreaker.

7. Make Way for Tomorrow

1937, directed by Leo McCarey. With Victor Moore, Beulah Bondi, Thomas Mitchell, Fay Bainter, Elisabeth Risdon, Porter Hall

Orson Welles declared, "It's a movie that could make a stone cry." After a series of bad financial decisions, an old married couple, Bark and Lucy, lose their house through foreclosure. Their children are either unable or unwilling to take them in together, and the only solution seems to be separation. They spend one last day together in Manhattan before saying good-bye. Echoing the effects of our current economic downturn, it was in fact made in 1937. As Lucy, Beulah Bondi (who played Jimmy Stewart's mom in *It's a Wonderful Life*) is simply magnificent. Incidentally, she was only 49 years old at the time.

8. Umberto D

1952, directed by Vittorio De Sica. With Carlo Battisti, Maria Pia Casilio, Lina Gennari, Ileana Simova

Having lost his pension, an elderly retired bureaucrat in Rome is about to be evicted from his tiny room at a boarding house and put out onto the streets. His only comfort is his little dog, Flike. How will they survive? To give away more details here is unthinkable. De Sica presents the story in as straightforward a manner as possible, using non-actors in the lead roles, sharpening the feeling of realism. I'm not even a dog lover (no *Old Yeller* on this list, you'll notice), and this movie still got to me. Equally touching is Umberto's friendship with Maria, the serving girl at the boarding house.

16

Great Movies Based on Plays

By Halley Feiffer

Halley Feiffer is a playwright and actress. She won the National Young Playwrights' Contest in 2002, and has appeared on stage in many productions. In April 2011, she made her Broadway debut in *The House of Blue Leaves*, which also starred Ben Stiller, Edie Falco, and Jennifer Jason Leigh. Her notable film roles include *You Can Count on Me*, *Stephanie Daley*, *The Squid and the Whale*, *Margot at the Wedding*, *The Messenger*, and Todd Haynes's miniseries *Mildred Pierce*. She narrates the Books on Tape recording of *Blubber*, by Judy Blume.

I love plays, and I love movies, and I love playwriting, and I love movie writing, and I love acting in plays, and I love acting in movies, and I love writing about all these things, so I wrote the following. Let me point out that this is by no means a comprehensive list; this is just a sampling of some favorites. So . . . *Curtain up!* I mean . . . *Action?* I mean . . .

1. Vanya on 42nd Street

1994, directed by Louis Malle. With Wallace Shawn, Andre Gregory, Julianne Moore, Larry Pine, Phoebe Brand, Lynn Cohen, George Gaynes, Jerry Mayer, Brooke Smith, Madhur Jaffrey

When I was asked to write a list of some of my favorite film adaptations of plays, this brilliant and bizarre work is the first thing that came to mind. I was shown this film as part of a Chekhov class I took freshman year of college, and it blew my little brain off and helped to win me over as a die-hard Chekhov fan. I have since ordered anyone who complains that Chekhov is "boring" and "about nothing" to run out and rent Louis Malle's ingenious, fly-on-the-wall capturing of a single rehearsal of Andre Gregory's staging of *Uncle Vanya*, translated by David Mamet. Renowned theater director Gregory has an unorthodox process of putting on a play: he gathers a couple friends together to any rehearsal space he can find (in this case, the abandoned New Amsterdam Theatre on 42nd Street), and they explore scenes from a play with no set performance date, no audience, and no real goal other than under-standing the text better and making some cool theater moments.

> "Something new. What's new? Nothing's new. Everything's old. Nothing's changed. I'm the same. Probably a little bit worse because I've grown lazy, complain all day."
>
> –VANYA, *VANYA ON 42ND STREET*

The opening credits roll as we follow the always-brilliant Wallace Shawn as he moseys through Times Square, pausing to buy a hotdog and munching on it as he enters the theater, where he joins his fellow collaborators for some casual chatting and styrofoam-cup-coffee-sipping. Then, before we're even really aware of it, rehearsal has begun, and we become flies on the wall, witnessing the intimate and jaw-droppingly gorgeous unfolding of this ingenious tragicomedy. Julianne Moore is perfect as Yelena, the enchanting and way-too-young second wife of an ancient professor; Larry Pine is devastating as Astrov, the charismatic alcoholic doctor who is infatuated with her; and the shattering Brooke Smith is Sonya, Yelena's plain daughter-in-law who is, of course, desperately head-over-heels for Astrov. And then there is Shawn, at once hilarious and heartbreaking as Vanya, the professor's nebbishy and vitriolic brother-in-law who is, of course, also in love with the bewitching Yelena. This is one of the few films, in my opinion, that captures the thrill of live theater—often better than some live theater I've seen!

2. Little Shop of Horrors

1986, directed by Frank Oz. With Rick Moranis, Ellen Greene, Vincent Gardenia, Steve Martin, Levi Stubbs, Bill Murray

What does it say about me that this musical tale of a bloodlusty giant plant was one of my favorite films as a child? As a kid whose fondest memory took place in the grotto at the Playboy Mansion (I'll explain another day), I guess not that much. But still, this film really left an impression. Rick Moranis was born to play Seymour, a drippy four-eyed loser who works in a down-and-out plant shop on Skid Row, run by the tyrannical and terrifying Mr. Mushnik. The only ray of sunshine in his pathetic life is his lovely-if-slatternly-dressed coworker Audrey, played to perfection by an adorable Ellen Greene. Things start to get complicated when Seymour discovers a new kind of plant—a Venus Flytrap–type thing—that starts to attract a ton of attention to the shop. The only catch? It eats blood. Only blood. Human blood. The supporting cast in Frank Oz's adaptation is as stellar as the film's stars: Steve Martin as the nitrous-addicted abusive dentist, Bill Murray as his masochistic patient, and keep your eyes peeled for Jim Belushi, John Candy, and Christopher Guest in cameo roles. I was thrilled when I was cast as a chorus member in my theater camp's production of *Little Shop,* and then horrified to learn that the ending of the stage version is . . . quite different. And much darker. And after I got over my horror? I was thrilled, again.

3. The Heiress

1949, directed by William Wyler. With Olivia de Havilland, Montgomery Clift, Ralph Richardson, Miriam Hopkins, Ray Collins

I was kind of nervous to include this picture on the list because it's a movie based on a play based on a book. Does that count? Eh, I don't care, it's so awesome, whatever, who cares, if you care, I don't like you, just kidding I probably do. Henry James's novel *Washington Square* is one of my favorite reads; it tells the tale of the wealthy, plain, and pathologically timid Catherine Sloper, who lives in a gorgeous brownstone in nineteenth-century New York under the oppressive thumb of her widower father, a brilliant doctor who views his ugly-duckling only child as a massive disappointment. When Catherine begins to find herself the object of admiration of the devastatingly charming rascal Morris Townsend, Dr. Sloper's bullshit meter buzzes, and he informs Catherine that she can expect not a penny from him if she marries the brownnosing Morris. When Morris is played by someone as disgustingly appealing as Montgomery Clift, Catherine's tragic inability to let him go is even more relatable. Olivia de Havilland's Oscar-winning performance as the pitiful Catherine is by turns wrenching and electrifying. And I still get chills recalling the film's final moment, which is sublimely spooky and exhilarating.

4. A Streetcar Named Desire

1951, directed by Elia Kazan. With Vivien Leigh, Marlon Brando, Kim Hunter, Karl Malden, Rudy Bond, Nick Dennis

You can't compile a list of favorite plays-turned-films without including Elia Kazan's masterpiece adaptation of his Broadway production of Tennessee Williams's stupidly amazing play. I pity any actor who has had to play Stanley Kowalski after watching Marlon Brando's animalistic turn as the thuggish and disgustingly sexy "Polack" who is married to the sister of our heroine (if you can call her that), the delicate-as-lace Southern belle Blanche DuBois. And Vivien Leigh is of course divine as the moth-like Blanche—she flutters around the Kowalski's cramped New Orleans apartment, stealthily trying to find liquor (just to calm her nerves, of course) as she trashes that brute of a husband her sister Stella decided to marry and turns the lives of everyone around her upside down with her seductive narcissism. Kim Hunter is fierce as the earthy Stella, and Karl Malden destroys me as Mitch, the poor sot who crushes hard on Blanche. The only qualm I have with the film is that (spoiler alert!) allusions to a certain character's homosexuality were removed and replaced with references to his "weakness." I know it was the '50s, but still . . .

5. Glengarry Glen Ross

1992, directed by James Foley. With Al Pacino, Jack Lemmon, Alec Baldwin, Ed Harris, Alan Arkin, Kevin Spacey, Jonathan Pryce

I guess David Mamet is a pretty good writer, because this is his second appearance on my list. The opening scene in the 2005 Broadway revival between Liev Schreiber and Alan Alda as foul-mouthed, rapid-tongued real estate agents had my head spinning and heart thumping. Alec Baldwin's delicious monologue as the sleazy motivational-speaker-type Blake in the film version is just as mesmerizing. There's also Al Pacino, Jack Lemmon, Kevin Spacey, Alan Arkin, Ed Harris, Jonathan Pryce—what a cast! I like women and being a woman and all that, but watching these guys verbally molest one another as the last shred of their humanity oozes out of them like air from a deflating balloon makes me wish I could make like a Mamet character and light up a cigar and jump on a barstool and morally flagellate all the broads I've slept with for an hour or two, too.

> "You know why, mister? 'Cause you drove a Hyundai to get here tonight, I drove an $80,000 BMW. . . . You can't play in the man's game, you can't close them, you go home and tell your wife your troubles. Because only one thing counts in this life: get them to sign on the line which is dotted."
>
> —BLAKE, *GLENGARRY GLEN ROSS*

Elliott Gould as apathetic photographer Alfred Chamberlain in *Little Murders*. Somebody named Jules Feiffer wrote the screenplay, based on his play.

6. **Little Murders**

1971, directed by Alan Arkin. With Elliott Gould, Marcia Rodd, Vincent Gardenia, Elizabeth Wilson, Donald Sutherland, Jon Korkes, Lou Jacobi, Doris Roberts, John Randolph

I guess Alan Arkin must be a pretty talented guy, too, because this is also his second time on my list. With this darkly hilarious dystopian family hellscape, however, Arkin wears the helmer's hat, making only a brief cameo appearance as the demented loony tune Lieutenant Practice. The twisted story centers on the Newquist family: Mrs. Newquist; her husband, Carol—YES, MEN CAN BE NAMED CAROL, TOO, HE'LL HAVE YOU KNOW; their toilet-talk-prone son, Kenny; and the apple of the family's eye: the stunning and all-around-all-star daughter, Patsy.

When Patsy brings home her new boyfriend, Alfred (the incredible Elliott Gould), for supper and they ask what exactly he does for a living . . . well, let's just say, the bullets flying through the windows of the Newquists' Upper West Side abode become the least of their problems. What kind of sick-brained sadist wrote this nutty nightmare? I don't know, and I hope I never meet him, 'cause this guy's messed up.

But if he wants to send me some money . . . that'd be cool.

17

Great Movies for
Tweens, Teens, and Other Kids
under the Age of 99

L et's face it: there are plenty of movies marketed for parents to watch with their kids, and most of them are completely unmemorable. They're either helplessly dull, assume the audience has an attention span of 3.5 seconds, or are so sickly bright and cheerful that anyone over the age of 12 is liable to run screaming from the room. So here are some movies perfect for sharing, with choices for elementary school–age children through tweens and teens. I speak from personal experience when I say that the best way to make sure your kids grow up with a taste for great movies is to get them started early. (Thanks, Mom and Dad!)

1. The Red Balloon

1956, directed by Albert Lamorisse. With Pascal Lamorisse, Georges Sellier, Vladimir Popov, Paul Perey, René Marion, Sabine Lamorisse, Michel Pezin

On his way to school one morning, a little boy (played by the director's son) discovers a red balloon tied to a lamppost. After freeing it, he quickly finds out the balloon has a mind of its own. Their series of adventures in a sun-dappled Paris forms the basis of this beautifully simple film, which won an Oscar for Best Original Screenplay despite an absence of dialogue. It's often paired with another charming film by the same filmmakers, *White Mane,* about a country boy who tames a wild horse. Trivia: Lamorisse also invented the board game Risk.

2. Yellow Submarine

1968, directed by George Dunning. Voices by Paul Angelis, John Clive, Dick Emery, Geoff Hughes, Lance Percival, Peter Batten

Aside from appearing briefly at the end, the Beatles themselves had little to do with this animated film, but it's certainly a worthy addition to their legacy. John, Paul, George, and Ringo rally to rout the music-hating Blue Meanies, who have banished all life and color from the kingdom of Pepperland. The movie stitches together about a dozen Beatles songs with a wild melange of animated techniques, in effect perfecting the music video form before such a thing even existed.

3. Gojira

1954, directed by Ishirô Honda. With Akira Takarada, Momoko Kôchi, Akihiko Hirata, Takashi Shimura, Fuyuki Murakami, Sachio Sakai, Ren Yamamoto

Tell the kids to put away their Transformers for a while and enjoy some rampaging monster action together. Title doesn't ring a bell? You may know it by its American name: *Godzilla.* (By the way, translated literally, *gojira* means "gorilla whale.") Everyone knows the story by now. Oceanic nuclear testing awakens the primeval monster Gojira from his underground cave, sending him ashore to wreak havoc on Japan. For the American release, the film was re-edited and stuffed with inserts of Raymond Burr playing a reporter named Steve Martin (!). The original Japanese version, now available on DVD, is a rather more somber tale. There's even an avant-garde music score with lots of clangs and shrieks. But it's oddly comforting to notice all the disaster movie archetypes making early appearances here: the eye patch–wearing mad scientist; the heroine, whose main purpose is to alternate between screaming and crying; the dumb hunk, who naturally gets the girl; the idealistic professor, who wants to study the beast; and the military man, who just wants to nuke it. Good fun for all ages.

4. Time Bandits

1981, directed by Terry Gilliam. With Craig Warnock, John Cleese, Sean Connery, Shelley Duvall, Ralph Richardson, Katherine Helmond, Ian Holm, Michael Palin, David Warner

A schoolboy discovers that his bedroom is one of many "time portals," holes in the space-time continuum. These holes are being exploited by a cadre of dwarves who hopscotch through history, stealing things along the way. It's all made possible by a map of the universe, which they've stolen from the Supreme Being. He understandably wants it back, but Evil wants to get his hands on it, too. Gleefully appropriating everything from *Alice in Wonderland* to *The Wizard of Oz*, Gilliam enlisted several of his pals from Monty Python to fill small roles (including Cleese, very funny as a smarmy, glad-handing Robin Hood). I have to confess that I was obsessed with this movie as a kid. I eventually watched it so many times on cable TV that my parents banned it from the household!

5. Sherlock Jr.

1924, directed by Buster Keaton. With Buster Keaton, Kathryn McGuire, Joe Keaton, Erwin Connelly, Ward Crane

If you're looking for the perfect way to introduce kids (and/or yourself) to classic silent cinema, you could do a lot worse than this masterpiece. The sad-eyed Buster created a film that was postmodern before "modern" even existed. He plays a

Buster Keaton in *Sherlock Jr.* In addition to directing, Keaton did all his own stunts in the movie, including hanging off a railroad water tank.

movie projectionist who eventually steps into the very movie he's showing, a detective mystery, in the process solving a crime that's taken place in the on-screen world. It's a hilarious movie that's also unexpectedly poignant, and it's been appropriated by countless filmmakers, including Luis Buñuel and Woody Allen.

6. An American in Paris

1951, directed by Vincente Minnelli. With Gene Kelly, Leslie Caron, Oscar Levant, Georges Guétary, Nina Foch

Ending with a beautiful seventeen-minute ballet sequence (there are at least eleven Gershwin tunes on the soundtrack), this Technicolor confection about some ex-pats in the City of Light is delightful no matter what your age. Of course it has nothing to do with the "real" Paris. This is the Paris of the movies: an artfully faux Paris, a fantasy Paris tricked out with candy-colored production design executed so skillfully even the bottles behind the bar in the café are fascinating. Oscar Levant (as cynical piano player Adam Cook)

> "It's not a pretty face, I grant you, but underneath its flabby exterior is an enormous lack of character. I like Paris. It's a place where you don't run into old friends, although that's never been one of my problems."
>
> —ADAM COOK, AN AMERICAN IN PARIS

steals every scene he's in—a particularly memorable dream sequence has him conducting an orchestra of his own doppelgängers.

7. Meet Me in St. Louis

1944, directed by Vincente Minnelli. With Judy Garland, Margaret O'Brien, Mary Astor, Lucille Bremer, Tom Drake, Marjorie Main, Leon Ames

Judy Garland slowly moves across the room to the window, gazing longingly into the distance as if imagining her future. She's singing "The Boy Next Door," a song captured by Minnelli's camera in a single take, and it's practically the movies' definitive statement on puppy love. This series of vignettes detailing a homespun American family's life, circa 1904—and their excitement about the upcoming Louisiana Purchase Exposition World's Fair—is pure magic. Margaret O'Brien, as Judy's kid sister Tootie, is too cute for words. Oh, yeah: this movie also introduced "Have Yourself a Merry Little Christmas." Here, the song has much darker lyrics than most later versions, including the line "Until then, we'll have to muddle through somehow . . ."

8. The River

1951, directed by Jean Renoir. With Patricia Walters, Nora Swinburne, Esmond Knight, Arthur Shields, Thomas E. Breen, Adrienne Corri, Suprova Mukerjee, Radha Burnier

Here's a film so vibrant and complex it makes most contemporary movies about childhood seem downright pallid. Harriet, "an ugly duckling trying to be a swan," grows up in Bengal on the banks of a mighty river. She's part of a cheerfully cacophonous household that includes her parents, four sisters, and one brother. A schoolgirl crush on Captain John, a battle-scarred World War II veteran who comes to stay with a neighbor, forms the backbone for one of the most exquisite color films ever made. Capturing the wonders, mysteries, and dangers of India, *The River* offers up moment after moment of beauty. The bustling bazaar, the celebration of Diwali (the Indian festival of lights), and a joyous wedding dance are only a few of the highlights. Incidentally, Wes Anderson credits it as the primary inspiration for *The Darjeeling Limited.*

9. The Train

1964, directed by John Frankenheimer. With Burt Lancaster, Paul Scofield, Jeanne Moreau, Michel Simon, Suzanne Flon, Jacques Marin

While I'm on the subject of trains . . . it's the height of World War II, and a train of stolen art treasures is bound for Nazi Germany. Can a rescue attempt by the Resistance be far behind? *Raiders of the Lost Ark* owes a huge debt to this exciting suspense thriller, and just like that film, *The Train* is a great movie for older kids and their parents to watch together. Aside from a cracking good story there's a lot to enjoy here, especially the film's razor-sharp black-and-white look, which favors the steam and grime of the title conveyance. Once you get past Lancaster playing a French stationmaster, all the actors acquit themselves nicely. A suitably existential ending is the capper.

10. Girls Town

1996, directed by Jim McKay. With Lili Taylor, Bruklin Harris, Aunjanue Ellis, Anna Grace, Guillermo Díaz

Three street-smart girls at an inner-city high school struggle to cope after a close friend inexplicably commits suicide. As graduation draws near, the teens find themselves dealing with their rage and future outlook in ways they never have before. This honest, nonjudgmental examination of urban adolescence is by turns funny and sobering. The dialogue was largely written out of workshop-style improvisation before shooting, and there isn't a false note to any of it. Lili Taylor, as the young mother and underachiever of the group, is simply wonderful (as always), but she's matched by Bruklin Harris and Anna Grace, who refuse to let themselves be taken for granted just because they're women. A challenging film for parents to watch with teens perhaps (there's some strong language), but this is the rare kind of film that inspires complex feelings without telling you how to feel. It can surely inspire a heartfelt conversation.

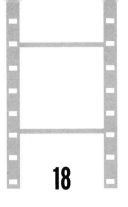

18

Fabulous Films for Young Adults

by the Young Adult Library Services Association

The Young Adult Library Services Association (YALSA) is a division of the American Library Association. A national association of librarians, library workers, and advocates, its mission is to expand and strengthen library services for young adults. Through its member-driven advocacy, research, and professional development initiatives, YALSA builds the capacity of libraries and librarians to engage, serve, and empower teens. The movies below are culled from their "Fabulous Films for Young Adults" lists, chosen annually to identify films that will appeal to those ages 12 through 18. I've roughly arranged them by level of maturity, chipping in my own thoughts along the way.

1. Ghost in the Shell

1995, directed by Mamoru Oshii. With Atsuko Tonaka, Iemasa Kayumi, Richard Epcar

A computer wants to hack into people's minds and take over their memories. Major Motoko Kusanagi vows to stop it in this pioneering cyberpunk anime. The fleet visual style matches the storyline, which hurtles along so fast you'll have a hard time keeping up with the plot. Don't let that worry you: like the best action movies, it's the momentum that counts.

2. Hairspray

1988, directed by John Waters. With Ricki Lake, Divine, Debbie Harry, Sonny Bono, Jerry Stiller, Leslie Ann Powers, Colleen Fitzpatrick, Michael St. Gerard, Ruth Brown, Mink Stole

From the future to the past: it's 1962, and watching *The Corny Collins Show* after school is *the* way to pick up on all the latest music and dance moves, from the Madison to the Roach and the Bug. Plus-sized teen Tracy Turnblad makes it her mission to become a regular on the

> "You've got something against Connie Francis? Shelley Fabares? I love Shelley Fabares. Amber? Amber, are you listening to me? We have to have a little talk. You know, if your father is forced to integrate Tilted Acres, we're out of business. So at least act white on television."
>
> —VELMA VON TUSSLE, *HAIRSPRAY*

show. Along the way her love for R&B inspires her to fight against the program's strictly segregated format. Racism is the ultimate form of tackiness in Waters's best film. He cannily mixes campy touches (like Blondie's Debbie Harry as a villainous stage mom Velma Von Tussle) with catchy songs. The tunes in the musical remake, which stars John Travolta and Zac Efron, can't touch the period originals included here, which include "Foot Stompin'" and "Nothing Compares to You."

3. Pleasantville

1998, directed by Gary Ross. With Tobey Maguire, Reese Witherspoon, Jeff Daniels, Joan Allen, William H. Macy, J. T. Walsh

Here's another film that looks at nostalgia with a contemporary eye. With the help of an enigmatic TV repairman (played by Don Knotts!), a brother and sister are magically transported through their television set and into the black-and-white world of a 1950s sitcom called *Pleasantville*. Soon they affect this environment with their worldly sensibilities, and people and things slowly begin to acquire color, their complacent lives profoundly changed.

4. An Education

2009, directed by Lone Scherfig. With Carey Mulligan, Peter Sarsgaard, Emma Thompson, Dominic Cooper, Olivia Williams, Alfred Molina, Rosamund Pike

Sixteen-year-old Jenny (Mulligan) is ready to be an adult. She meets an older man who introduces her to the colorful world of Britain in the 1960s. As she becomes more entranced with his lifestyle, she has to come to some decisions about her own future. The film made Mulligan a star, and it isn't hard to see why. She's effortlessly charming. Sarsgaard is also marvelous, somehow de-creepifying the notion of a 30-something guy dating a teenager.

5. Persepolis

2007, directed by Marjane Satrapi and Vincent Paronnaud. With the voices of Gena Rowlands, Sean Penn, Iggy Pop, Amethyste Frezignac, Lexie Kendrick, Aoife Stone

Based on Satrapi's graphic novel, this animated feature chronicles the coming of age of a spirited young Iranian girl during the Islamic Revolution. It offers a visually dazzling picture of life in Iran that's vastly more complex than anything you might see on the evening news.

6. Osama

2003, directed by Siddiq Barmak. With Marina Golbahari, Arif Herati, Zubaida Sahar, Khwaja Nader

Another slice of life from the Middle East, *Osama* is a film you won't soon forget. Being female in Taliban-controlled Afghanistan is difficult, but when Osama's mother

The original French version of *Persepolis,* featuring the voices of Catherine Deneuve and her daughter Chiara Mastroianni, is also available on video.

decides to pass her off as a male, and her real identity is discovered, her life turns tragic. The first movie produced in Afghanistan after the defeat of the Taliban, this simple film gradually builds to a shattering conclusion.

7. Sunrise over Tiananmen Square

1998, directed by Shui-Bo Wang

Shui-Bo Wang combines his own artwork with family photos and archival material to present a personal and impressionistic view of China from the nineteenth century to the 1989 student massacre. On DVD it's paired with two other Oscar-nominated shorts: *Hardwood,* filmmaker Hubert Davis's portrait of his father, a Harlem Globetrotter; and *Ryan,* about a former animator's downfall.

8. Dogtown and Z-Boys

2001, directed by Stacy Peralta. Narrated by Sean Penn

This documentary captures the heyday of skateboarding in the west Los Angeles surfing community known as Dogtown during the 1970s. Peralta spotlights the quintessential skaters, known as the Z-Boys, who transformed the sport and popular culture.

9. Donnie Darko

2001, directed by Richard Kelly. With Jake Gyllenhaal, Jena Malone, Mary McDonnell,
Holmes Osborne, Katharine Ross, Maggie Gyllenhaal, Drew Barrymore, Patrick Swayze, Noah Wyle

An edgy, psychological thriller about a suburban teen who struggles to figure out where he fits in and comes face-to-face with his dark destiny. Donnie Darko (a spot-on Jake Gyllenhaal) is a delusional high-school student visited by a demonic rabbit with eerie visions of the past and deadly predictions for the future. Swayze is amusing as a screwy motivational speaker.

10. Dazed and Confused

1993, directed by Richard Linklater. With Jason London, Rory Cochrane, Wiley Wiggins,
Adam Goldberg, Matthew McConaughey, Kim Krizan, Parker Posey, Milla Jovovich, Ben Affleck

Parents may cringe at some of the behavior in *Dazed and Confused*. But teens will be teens, no matter what year it is. Here, it's 1976 in Texas and the last day of high school before the hazy days of summer commence. Naturally the day's activities include the hazing of the freshmen girls (hilariously undertaken by Posey) and—after dark—cruising around in cars, an impromptu keg party, and liberal use of marijuana. Linklater captures the time and place to a tee, and it's fun to see early performances from so many future stars.

11. Triumph of the Nerds: The Rise of Accidental Empires

1996, written and hosted by Robert X. Cringely

Told in three parts, this funny and engrossing documentary details how adolescent computer nerds Bill Gates and Steve Jobs evolved from amateurs working out of their bedrooms and garages to billionaires in the personal computer industry they helped to create. And just think of everything that's happened in the world of computers since this documentary was made!

19

Movies on My Mind

By Julia Sweeney

Julia Sweeney was a cast member of *Saturday Night Live* from 1990 to 1994. In addition to appearing in such films as *Pulp Fiction, Gremlins 2: The New Batch*, and *Clockstoppers*, she has garnered much acclaim for her stage monologues. They include *God Said, "Ha!"* (which she adapted and directed for film in 1999), *In the Family Way*, and *Letting Go of God*. She has frequently appeared as a panelist on the NPR news quiz radio show *Wait Wait . . . Don't Tell Me!* She blogs at juliasweeney.com.

1. The Trouble with Angels

1966, directed by Ida Lupino. With Rosalind Russell, Hayley Mills, June Harding, Mary Wickes, Marge Redmond, Camilla Sparv, Binnie Barnes, Judith Lowry, Gypsy Rose Lee

This is a great coming-of-age story, and a great spiritual story, and a great women's story, directed by one of the first great female directors: Ida Lupino. The scene where Hayley Mills watches Rosalind Russell mourn the loss of her friend is one of the most poignant and meaningful scenes I've ever seen.

2. The Naked Spur

1953, directed by Anthony Mann. With James Stewart, Janet Leigh, Robert Ryan, Ralph Meeker, Millard Mitchell

This is a wonderful Western, with astonishing performances by Jimmy Stewart as well as Janet Leigh and Robert Ryan. No one is purely good, and things get complicated. My favorite Western by Anthony Mann.

3. **Once upon a Time in Anatolia**

2011, directed by Nuri Bilge Ceylan. With Muhammet Uzuner, Yılmaz Erdoğan, Taner Birsel, Ahmet Mümtaz Taylan, Fırat Tanış

This Turkish film is haunting, existential, and mercilessly slow, but ultimately mesmerizing and heartbreaking and beautiful. There are shots that are long. Really long. Almost-to-the-point-of-parody long. But it's necessary—you begin to feel you're with the characters in real time. In the middle of the night. Driving around the countryside of Turkey. Looking for a dead body. With little or no information about who it is, how he died, why it's important, and who the hell everyone who's looking for him is, exactly. And guess what, it turns out that it actually isn't all that important—the who, how, and why. My favorite movie from 2011.

4. **The Shop around the Corner**

1940, directed by Ernst Lubitsch. With Margaret Sullavan, James Stewart, Frank Morgan, Joseph Schildkraut, Sara Haden, Felix Bressart, William Tracy

There isn't a false frame in this entire film. The whole thing is perfection, and I watch this every year at Christmastime. In fact, I think it's required Christmas viewing. For the record, I've never seen the remake, *You've Got Mail*. I'm just too afraid that my beloved movie has been mangled.

5. **Days of Heaven**

1978, directed by Terrence Malick. With Richard Gere, Brooke Adams, Sam Shepard, Linda Manz

Nature is a character in this film (as it is in all Malick's films), and this is the one that makes the point-of-view of Nature most devastatingly. I have such happy memories of this film. I saw it when I was in college. I sat in the movie theater for some time afterward, just absorbing what I saw. And yet, the film is even better than I could have understood at the time. It gets better every time I see it.

6. **The River**

1951, directed by Jean Renoir. With Patricia Walters, Nora Swinburne, Esmond Knight, Arthur Shields, Thomas E. Breen, Adrienne Corri, Suprova Mukerjee, Radha Burnier

This film is more like a book, or a poem than a film, but I don't mean to detract from the visual feast to be had watching it. It's the first color film made in India. It's a young girl coming-of-age story (I guess I like those . . .) that's heartbreaking and sweet and real and sad—the film is a meditation on time. Fantastic. [*Rob's note:* See also chapter 17, "Great Movies for Tweens, Teens, and Other Kids under the Age of 99" for additional thoughts on *The River*.]

Once upon a Time in Anatolia won the Grand Prix at the 2011 Cannes Film Festival.

7. Daisy Kenyon

1947, directed by Otto Preminger. With Joan Crawford, Henry Fonda, Dana Andrews, Ruth Warrick, Peggy Ann Garner

Crawford and Fonda star in this love triangle that could have so easily been shot like a soap opera, but instead it's intelligent and insightful and surprisingly modern. It's my favorite Joan Crawford performance.

8. It's Always Fair Weather

1955, directed by Stanley Donen and Gene Kelly. With Gene Kelly, Dan Dailey, Cyd Charisse, Michael Kidd, Dolores Gray, David Burns

This is a great, dark, sad, yet weirdly hopeful postwar musical with amazing dancing and a terrific Cyd Charisse. Should we just say, categorically, that Cyd Charisse has the best body ever on film? Maybe ever in the history of women? I think so. I think she's the best dancer, too.

9. White Light/Black Rain: The Destruction of Hiroshima and Nagasaki

2007, directed by Steven Okazaki

This film takes you a long way toward understanding the real effect the atomic bombs had on people who survived. I can't stop flashing on their stories from this film. Okazaki was able to shoot many of their stories just before they died. I swear, some of the descriptions and scenes are images I flash on every day. Everyone should see this film. It's not unhopeful, and it's not a complete downer, so don't let the subject matter scare you away. Just astonishing.

10. Salesman

1969, directed by Albert and David Maysles, and Charlotte Zwerin

This is a documentary about Catholic Bible salesmen. The footage was shot in 1966–67. We follow four or five guys and see how their day-to-day lives are lived. It's tragic, funny, odd, and a complete time-grab from that era of housewives and curlers and people struggling to make a living. The main guy (or the person who turns into the main guy, I should say) is a Willy Loman–like, sweet, manipulative person who's hitting the ceiling on his abilities to sell and keep himself together. It's a view of the world in 1967 that is discombobulatingly authentic and visceral. I think of this film all the time. Once you see it, you will become a big fan of the Maysles brothers' films and will want to see all of them. But this one is definitely the best.

20

Nine Movies for Lively Discussions

The old saying goes that if two people ever agree on everything, one of them isn't necessary. Very good (and bad) movies can often be polarizing. Some of the best movie experiences of my life have been those that led to some spirited conversation afterward. Here are some movies that may get you talking even before the end credits roll.

1. Irréversible

2002, directed by Gaspar Noé. With Monica Bellucci, Vincent Cassel, Albert Dupontel, Jo Prestia, Mourad Khimaand

One of the most controversial films of recent times, Irréversible makes it impossible to walk away indifferent. Like Memento, this movie unfolds in reverse chronology. Beginning (ending) with a bloody act of revenge, the story progresses backward and we gradually discover the reasons behind it. The movie features graphic violence galore, but it's the disturbing scene of sexual brutality at the heart of the movie that really divides moviegoers. Thus, Irréversible is either a "a genuine outlaw work of art" (Stephen Hunter, Washington Post) or "an exploitation movie with a gimmick, not to mention a vacuous philosophy" (J. Hoberman, Village Voice).

2. **Psycho**

1998, directed by Gus Van Sant. With Vince Vaughn, Anne Heche, Julianne Moore, Viggo Mortensen, William H. Macy, Philip Baker Hall

When Van Sant announced that he'd be doing a shot-for-shot remake of the Hitchcock classic, reactions ranged from outrage to confusion and even admiration. The result is not an exact duplicate, strictly speaking: it's in color, has different camera angles, and some new dialogue (including the decidedly non-1960 line "Let me get my Walkman.") Frankly, I think this movie is an affront, but it does have its passionate defenders, including *New York Times* film critic Janet Maslin, who praises it as an "artful, good-looking remake . . . that shrewdly revitalizes the aspects of the real *Psycho.*"

3. **Kurt and Courtney**

1998, directed by Nick Broomfield

Documentary bad boy Broomfield explores the theory that Courtney Love was responsible for the death of her husband, Nirvana frontman Kurt Cobain. In the process he meets an assortment of weirdos and lowlifes, including a rumored hit man named El Duce. Your reaction to the claims made in the movie will probably depend on your opinion of Courtney Love herself. Famously, the Sundance Film Festival canceled a scheduled screening after her lawyers intervened.

All dressed alike and never given names, the characters in *Last Year at Marienbad* seem nearly interchangeable. Writer Alain Robbe-Grillet and director Alain Resnais's cool enigma will either hypnotize you or act like a good sleeping pill.

4. Last Year at Marienbad

1961, directed by Alain Resnais. With Delphine Seyrig, Giorgio Albertazzi, Sacha Pitoëff

A large group of the idle rich, whose names we never learn, pass their days at an enormous chateau, wandering the grounds or playing an enigmatic game of strategy called Nim. Among them is a man who repeatedly insists that he met one of the women last year at Marienbad, "or perhaps at Fredericksburg." That's about the extent of the plot—the movie is really an examination of time's slippery nature, with Resnais's smoothly gliding camera undertaking a slow exploration of the environment and the characters. The past, present, and future all coexist in a twilight world between dreams and reality. With its Coco Chanel fashions and baffling structure, it was one of the most hotly debated movies of its day. Chances are you'll walk away either completely enthralled or thoroughly annoyed.

5. Birth

2004, directed by Jonathan Glazer. With Nicole Kidman, Cameron Bright, Danny Huston, Lauren Bacall, Alison Elliott, Arliss Howard, Anne Heche, Peter Stormare

Kidman plays Anna, whose husband (Huston) suddenly dies. Ten years later, a young boy appears on the doorstep of her Manhattan highrise apartment, claiming to be her husband. Is he really the man's reincarnation, or just a kid who's been coached to say the right things? Set in the rarefied world of upper class luxury, this sleek puzzler stretches its central mystery to the breaking point and is the kind of movie that encourages you to tease out its clues afterward. Kidman and Huston are superb in difficult roles, and Bacall lights up her every scene as Kidman's disapproving mother.

6. The Rapture

1991, directed by Michael Tolkin. With Mimi Rogers, David Duchovny, Will Patton, Darwyn Carson, Patrick Bauchau

Rogers plays a woman living an empty, self-absorbed lifestyle who experiences a spiritual awakening and turns to God. As she becomes ever more deeply involved in the religious fundamentalism of her new church, signs begin to mount that the apocalypse is nigh. As Leonard Maltin writes, "This much-debated film truly rushes in where virtually no others have dared to tread." Writer/director Tolkin plays everything that happens with complete sincerity, daring the audience to take everything literally. His approach gives real impact to a story that could otherwise feel outlandish. Be prepared for on-screen carnage, matter-of-fact appearances by angels, and a genuinely disturbing ending.

7. White Dog

1982, directed by Samuel Fuller. With Kristy McNichol, Paul Winfield, Burl Ives, Jameson Parker

A young woman takes in a stray German Shepherd, never suspecting that it's a "white dog": a dog trained to attack blacks. After the dog's behavior is tragically revealed, African American animal trainer Winfield makes it his mission to deprogram the animal. Legendary filmmaker Fuller pulls no punches in this incisive examination of racism, implying that racial hatred can be unlearned. Ironically *White Dog* was the target of a prerelease boycott campaign by the NAACP, whose representatives (never having seen the film) claimed that it denigrated blacks. After a limited release in Europe, Paramount shelved it altogether. Fuller never made an another American movie.

8. Lake of Fire

2007, directed by Tony Kaye

In this often impressionistic documentary, Kaye exhaustively lays out the arguments and perspectives of those on all sides of the abortion debate, talking with public figures like Noam Chomsky, Alan Dershowitz, Peter Singer, and Randall Terry. He also speaks with numerous average Americans; what's on-screen is by turns thought provoking, graphic, and maddening. No matter where your beliefs lie, you're likely to come away from the movie with a new understanding of the issues involved.

9. The Power of Nightmares

2004, directed by Adam Curtis

This audacious three-part essay which premiered on the BBC posits that the so-called War on Terror is simply an elaborate, cynical ploy to justify endless war. Beginning with a biography of radical Arabic thinker Sayyid Qutb, whose short sojourn in 1950s Colorado inspired a violent disgust with the Western world, Curtis traces the evolution of

> "Instead of delivering dreams, politicians now promise to protect us. From nightmares."
>
> —ADAM CURTIS,
> *THE POWER OF NIGHTMARES*

radicalism in the Middle East. He shows how it paralleled the rise of the neoconservative movement in the United States, setting the two on an inevitable collision course. Some viewers will feel a certain vindication in Curtis's theories; others will cry foul. Curtis's examination of propaganda, which touches on issues of censorship, makes for a perfect segue to chapter 21, "DIY First Amendment Film Festival."

21

DIY First Amendment Film Festival

by the American Library Association's
Office for Intellectual Freedom

E stablished in 1967, the American Library Association's Office for Intellectual Freedom's goal is to educate librarians and the general public about the nature and importance of intellectual freedom—the freedom to access information and express ideas, even if the information and ideas might be considered unorthodox or unpopular—in libraries. It does this through initiatives such as Banned Books Week, an annual event celebrating the freedom to read and the importance of the First Amendment; and privacyrevolution.org, which aims to spark a national conversation about privacy rights in a digital age. The list below is compiled from a Banned Books Week resource guide, spiced up with some additional observations by yours truly.

1. Fahrenheit 451

1966, directed by François Truffaut. With Julie Christie, Oskar Werner, Cyril Cusack, Anton Diffring

Based upon the Ray Bradbury novel, this sci-fi drama depicts a future totalitarian and oppressive society, where books are forbidden and the mission of firemen is to burn books. The movie's genuinely odd atmosphere can be attributed in part to the international makeup of the production: Truffaut spoke virtually no English,

Julie Christie has a dual role in *Fahrenheit 451*, playing both the zombie-like wife of Werner's fireman and a rebellious schoolteacher who reads books in defiance of the law. She's great in both parts.

making directing the film a challenge; Werner has a thick German accent; and virtually all the other actors are British. One of Bernard Herrmann's most haunting scores and stunning cinematography by Nicolas Roeg make this worthwhile.

2. The First Amendment Project

2004, directed by Chris Hegedus and Nick Doob

Taking freedom of speech as its collected theme, this series of short films offers a snapshot of life at the start of the twenty-first century and commentary on the erosion of First Amendment rights. Topics include the lawsuit filed against satirist Al Franken by Fox News for using their slogan in his book *Lies and the Lying Liars Who Tell Them: A Fair and Balanced Look at the Right;* New Jersey poet laureate Amiri Baraka's account of the battles he encountered over his 9/11-themed poem "Somebody Blew Up America"; and a consideration of the public's right to protest versus the need for security, set against the backdrop of the 2004 Republican National Convention.

3. The People vs. Larry Flynt

1996, directed by Miloš Forman. With Woody Harrelson, Courtney Love, Edward Norton, Richard Paul, James Cromwell, Donna Hanover, Crispin Glover, Vincent Schiavelli

Forman and screenwriters Scott Alexander and Larry Karaszewski offer up a surprisingly sympathetic portrayal of Larry Flynt, the publisher of *Hustler* magazine. The focus is on his struggle to make a living publishing his girlie magazine and how it changes into a battle for freedom of speech, culminating in his defense on charges of libel brought against him by the Reverend Jerry Falwell.

4. The Front

1976, directed by Martin Ritt. With Woody Allen, Zero Mostel, Herschel Bernardi, Michael Murphy, Andrea Marcovicci, Remak Ramsay, Lloyd Gough

Senator Joseph McCarthy took it upon himself to root out supposed Communists in the US government, and it was only the most egregious example of many anti-Communist witch hunts during the Cold War. The House of Representatives had their own initiative, the House Committee on Un-American Activities (HUAC), which investigated the Hollywood film industry. Taking a rare acting role in a film he didn't direct, Woody Allen plays a man of no real talent or strong political convictions who is paid to be a front for a group of blacklisted Hollywood writers who are no longer able to submit work under their own names. A political innocent, he starts to see the evils of the blacklist and how it destroys people and careers. He wants to take a stand—but how can he? Though most of the film is a sobering indictment of the treatment of those on the blacklist, there's also a riotous scene where Allen stonewalls a Congressional committee.

5. Good Night, and Good Luck.

2005, directed by George Clooney. With David Strathairn, George Clooney, Robert Downey Jr., Patricia Clarkson, Frank Langella, Jeff Daniels, Tate Donovan, Ray Wise

This riveting docudrama depicts the effort by television broadcast journalists Edward R. Murrow and Fred Friendly to expose the fearmongering tactics of Senator Joseph McCarthy. Not only an examination of McCarthyism, the film also provides a glimpse into the world of television news in its infancy, before the era of cable news networks. The action is punctuated by scenes with jazz singer Dianne Reeves fronting a small combo.

6. The Insider

1999, directed by Michael Mann. With Al Pacino, Russell Crowe, Renee Olstead, Christopher Plummer, Diane Venora, Philip Baker Hall, Lindsay Crouse, Gina Gershon, Michael Gambon

A tale from another era at CBS News, circa 1995, when the network silenced Lowell Bergman, its own producer, and Jeffrey Wigand, a former tobacco executive who revealed that the tobacco industry knew that cigarettes are addictive and harmful. The film depicts the pair's attempt to overcome the tobacco companies' and CBS's attempts to suppress Wigand's testimony.

7. Smothered: The Censorship Struggles of the Smothers Brothers Comedy Hour

2002, directed by Maureen Muldaur

More CBS! This engrossing documentary details the tribulations of Tommy and Dick Smothers and their popular late-'60s CBS television show. Their jabs at censorship, gun ownership, and the Vietnam War—considered controversial at the time—seem mild today, but still made television executives nervous and led to the show's cancellation.

8. Footloose

1984, directed by Herbert Ross. With Kevin Bacon, Lori Singer, Dianne Wiest, John Lithgow, Chris Penn, Sarah Jessica Parker

Who knew that a movie about censorship could be so rockin'? Filled with 1980s pop chestnuts, the original 1984 film details the life of a city boy who moves to a

As dedicated projectionist Alfredo in Cinema Paradiso, *Philippe Noiret contributes a heartwarming performance.*

small town where rock music and dancing have been banned; he decides to stand up to the town and rallies his classmates to fight for the right to hold a senior prom with music and dance. Everybody cut, everybody cut.

9. Pump Up the Volume

1990, directed by Allan Moyle. With Christian Slater, Samantha Mathis, Mimi Kennedy, Scott Paulin, Cheryl Pollak, Annie Ross, Ellen Greene

Behind the microphone the shy teenager Mark (Slater) transforms into "Hard Harry," the DJ of a pirate radio station whose uncensored commentary challenging the status quo infuriates the local high school principal. After one of the station's listeners commits suicide, a hunt for the pirate DJ starts, and he ends up in jail. When he calls on other teens to "seize the air," they follow his example.

10. Cinema Paradiso

1988, directed by Giuseppe Tornatore. With Philippe Noiret, Salvatore Cascio, Marco Leonardi, Jacques Perrin, Antonella Attili

A subtle tale that explores the unacceptability of censorship. The Cinema Paradiso is the only theatre in a small, suffocating Sicilian village, where the local priest expurgates all the love scenes from the movies, which are hung as strips of film in the projectionist's booth. The projectionist, Alfredo, befriends Toto, a local boy who grows up to take Alfredo's job until Alfredo tells Toto to leave because "you will never find your life in so narrow-minded a place." When Toto returns for Alfredo's funeral many years later, he receives a gift that Alfredo left for him: a movie reel, on which are all the expurgated scenes from the movies of his childhood—all the censored kisses, passion, and life.

22

Point of Order
Riveting Movies about the Law

There's a reason that TV schedules are dominated by cop shows and lawyer shows. The machinery of justice, with its labyrinthine laws and procedures, makes an ideal template for all kinds of stories, dramas as well as comedies. Here's a cross-section worth watching.

1. Adam's Rib

1949, directed by George Cukor. With Spencer Tracy, Katharine Hepburn, Judy Holliday, Tom Ewell, David Wayne, Jean Hagen, Hope Emerson, Marvin Kaplan

When a housewife busts in on her husband with another woman and starts taking potshots, it's an open-and-shut case of attempted murder. Right? Not when Spencer Tracy is the assistant DA and Katharine Hepburn is the defense attorney. The barrage of smart quips never lets up in this classic courtroom comedy, and its observations about the differences (and similarities) between men and women haven't aged a day. My favorite scene has Tracy demonstrating that men are perfectly capable of crying on demand. Kaplan has a great bit as a court stenographer with a very Noo Yawk accent.

2. Anatomy of a Murder

1959, directed by Otto Preminger. With James Stewart, Lee Remick, Ben Gazzara, Arthur O'Connell, George C. Scott, Joseph N. Welch, Eve Arden

Stewart plays a small-town lawyer who holds his cards close to the vest while simultaneously defending an Army hothead (Gazzara) on a murder charge and resisting the advances of the defendant's seductive wife (Remick). Arguably Preminger's greatest achievement, it's a film that's both expansive (with a running time of 160 minutes) and tightly wound. Preminger chose to shoot on location in Michigan's Upper Peninsula; but in typically perverse fashion, he mostly restricts the action to interiors. It's his talkiest film, yet also his most suspenseful, and was controversial at the time of its release for the frank discussion of sex and rape. It's also notable for the muscular jazz score by Duke Ellington, who cameos as a piano player named Pie-Eye (and even plays with Stewart in one scene!).

3. I Am a Fugitive from a Chain Gang

1932, directed by Mervyn LeRoy. With Paul Muni, Glenda Farrell, Helen Vinson, Noel Francis, Preston Foster, Allen Jenkins, Berton Churchill, Edward Ellis, David Landau, Sally Blane

James Allen is not a fugitive from justice. Justice is a fugitive from him. A World War I vet, he's in the wrong place at the wrong time during a robbery. He's quickly arrested, found guilty, and sentenced to ten years' hard labor. Then he makes a break for it and escapes to Chicago, hiding his background and eventually achieving great success in the construction business. But it's only a matter of time before his past catches up with him. To anyone who thinks that 1930s Hollywood fare was limited to elaborate Busby Berkeley musicals and slick screwball comedies, this raw, hard-hitting melodrama about selective equality under the law serves as an eye-opener. The finale will haunt you for days.

4. Judgment at Nuremberg

1961, directed by Stanley Kramer. With Spencer Tracy, Burt Lancaster, Richard Widmark, Marlene Dietrich, Judy Garland, Maximilian Schell, Montgomery Clift, William Shatner

This powerful courtroom movie dramatizes the post–World War II trials held in Nuremberg, specifically the case against a German judge (Lancaster) who is charged with crimes against humanity for his rulings during the Nazi era. In one of his last great roles, Tracy plays the tribunal's chief justice. Knotty issues of culpability and responsibility are masterfully explored in Abby Mann's Oscar-winning screenplay, brought to life by a powerhouse cast, including Schell (who also took home an Oscar) as the articulate defense attorney.

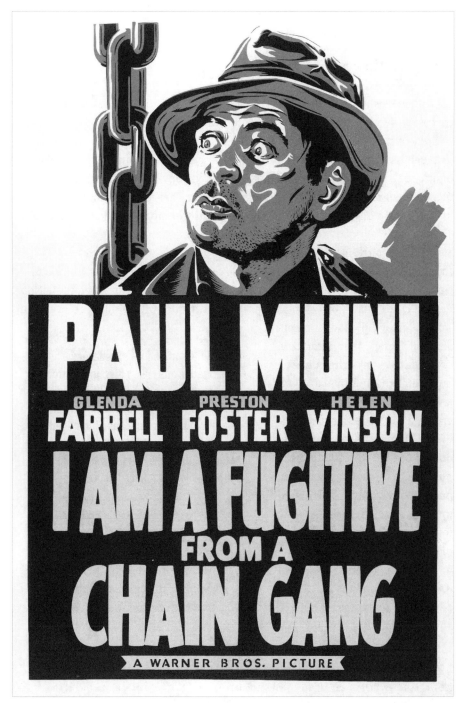

I Am a Fugitive from a Chain Gang was one of several "socially conscious" movies released by Warner Bros. in the 1930s. Others included *Black Legion*, about a Ku Klux Klan-like group, which starred Humphrey Bogart, and *Fury*, about a bloodthirsty lynch mob, with Spencer Tracy.

5. Tenth District Court

2004, directed by Raymond Depardon

This audaciously simple documentary observes various defendants as they appear in court before Michèle Bernard-Requin, a Parisian judge. Consisting almost entirely of close-ups, the expressions on the faces of the defendants tell the stories as much as their spoken testimony. They range from a woman who displays an enormous sense of entitlement despite repeated convictions for drunk driving, to illegal immigrants arrested on drug and violence charges. Though it's the French justice system on-screen, the proceedings feel surprisingly familiar.

6. The Trials of Henry Kissinger

2002, directed by Eugene Jarecki. Narrated by Brian Cox

Humorist Tom Lehrer once said, "Satire died the day that Kissinger won the Nobel Peace Prize." Taking place entirely in the courtroom of the viewer's mind, this "movie essay" uses documents, archival footage, and interviews with the likes of writer Christopher Hitchens and human rights lawyer Geoffrey Robertson to craft a basic indictment of Kissinger's foreign policy wrangling during the late '60s and '70s. It purports to uncover his fingerprints on everything from delaying the Vietnam Peace Accords for seven years (costing hundreds of thousands of lives) to encouraging the Indonesian genocide in East Timor, the Cambodian genocide of the Khmer Rouge, and the murderous coup of democratically elected President Allende of Chile on September 11, 1973. This provocative movie provokes and fascinates in equal measure.

> "Well if I ask myself why I began my investigation into Henry Kissinger, it would go back as far as when I realized that he was a frightened man. Because I became aware that he was personally frightened by the consequences of the arrest of General Pinochet. When the news of that hit, he instantly thought, 'Could I be next?'"
>
> —CHRISTOPHER HITCHENS, *THE TRIALS OF HENRY KISSINGER*

7. 12 Angry Men

1957, directed by Sidney Lumet. With Henry Fonda, Lee J. Cobb, E. G. Marshall, Martin Balsam, Jack Warden, John Fiedler, Jack Klugman, Edward Binns, Joseph Sweeney, Ed Begley

A very hot day, the end of a seemingly straightforward trial, a jury room with no air conditioning, and twelve sweaty jurors who would like nothing better than to reach a verdict as soon as possible. It's a murder case, a teenager accused of stabbing his father to death, and there are apparent eyewitnesses as well as several pieces of evidence. So why does Juror Number 8 (Fonda) refuse to go along with a verdict of "guilty"? Building from a celebrated teleplay by Reginald Rose that was originally performed and broadcast live on *Studio One,* Lumet uses the claustrophobia of the jury room to great effect, essentially turning the audience into juror Number 13. No one should mistake *12 Angry Men* for realism (the cast of supporting actors certainly dig into their meaty character parts with relish), but as a stylized look at the concept of American justice it's gripping stuff. Lumet would go on to make several courtroom dramas, including a look at justice from the other side of the bench in *The Verdict.*

8. **The Verdict**

1982, directed by Sidney Lumet. With Paul Newman, Charlotte Rampling, Jack Warden, James Mason, Milo O'Shea

Bluntly stated, the two greatest movies in the "has-been lawyer takes on a case in a last-ditch attempt to redeem himself" genre are *Anatomy of a Murder* and *The Verdict.* Whereas the former is leavened with a wry sense of humor, thanks to Jimmy Stewart's hem-hawing, Eve Arden's wisecracks, and Lee Remick as languorous sex kitten, *The Verdict* is most often chilly and cerebral—and no less fascinating for it. Every character is a "type," a mere cog in the plot's machinery: a lawyer on the

Lee J. Cobb in *12 Angry Men.* His character is known only as Juror Number 3.

skids (Newman); his gruff former partner (Warden); an icily sensual woman that Frank meets at a local bar (Rampling); the presiding judge who plays things strictly by the book (O'Shea). But James Mason, as the high-priced, press-savvy counsel for the defense, is the film's secret weapon. No one else could have played such a ruthless and rapacious lawyer with such mysterious dignity and grace; he steals every scene he's in. Look fast for Bruce Willis as a courtroom spectator.

23

Fifteen Favorite
Late-Night Spooky Films

By Barry Gifford

Essays on these films may be found in Barry Gifford's books *Out of the Past: Adventures in Film Noir* (2001) and *The Cavalry Charges* (2007). His books include *Sailor and Lula: The Complete Novels* (2010), of which David Lynch filmed *Wild at Heart*; *Night People* (1992); *Memories from a Sinking Ship* (2007); and *Sad Stories of the Death of Kings* (2010). He has written screenplays for numerous films, including *Lost Highway*, *Perdita Durango*, *City of Ghosts*, and *The Phantom Father*.

Rob's note > Barry Gifford, founder of Black Lizard (an imprint that has reprinted several classics of noir fiction) as well as a seasoned tale-spinner of the darkest human impulses, is well acquainted with things that go bump in the night. I asked him to name some of his favorite movies to watch 'round midnight, and here's what he chose (with annotations from me).

1. The Cabinet of Dr. Caligari

1920, directed by Robert Wiene. With Werner Krauss, Conrad Veidt, Friedrich Fehér, Lil Dagover, Hans Heinrich von Twardowski

According to Gifford: "The invention of film noir."

This silent classic epitomizes German Expressionism, an art film movement depicting extreme states of being using bizarre visuals, tilted camera angles, and unrealistic acting. The basic plot concerns the sinister Dr. Caligari, who travels with a circus in the guise of a magician, all the while wielding total control over his hypnotized slave, Cesare. The story is a springboard for the use of fantastic, exaggerated sets and makeup, and some supremely creepy moments involving the zombielike Cesare. As Gifford points out, with its painted sets and deep shadows it's a direct precursor to the sinister tales of desperate men and women gone bad that would later be called film noir.

2. Nosferatu

1922, directed by F. W. Murnau. With Max Schreck, Gustav von Wangenheim, Greta Schröder, Alexander Granach, Ruth Landshoff, Wolfgang Heinz

According to Gifford: "The über vampire flick."

If this silent film didn't exactly invent the movie vampire, it certainly crystallized a number of vampire motifs that are still with us today: rats, skeletons, the idea that vampires are killed by sunlight, and a character's discovery of neck punctures are but a few. Schreck's vampire, with his rodentlike teeth and wickedly long fingernails, remains iconic, even inspiring a fictional "making of" movie called *The Shadow of the Vampire,* with Willem Dafoe as Schreck. Trivia: after a court ruling that the movie constituted an unauthorized adaptation of Bram Stoker's *Dracula,* all copies were ordered destroyed. Luckily there were already a few prints of the film abroad, which is how *Nosferatu* has survived.

3. Island of Lost Souls

1932, directed by Erle C. Kenton. With Charles Laughton, Richard Arlen, Leila Hyams, Bela Lugosi, Kathleen Burke

According to Gifford: "Big nod to H. G. Wells. Charles Laughton at his campiest."

Based on H. G. Wells's novel *The Island of Dr. Moreau,* this surprisingly grisly tale of a mad scientist's medical experiments features a scenery-chewing turn by Laughton as the wacked-out doc. But a menagerie of grotesque half-human creatures almost steals the show. Most memorable is Lugosi, who utters the infamous line known to Devo fans everywhere: "Are we not men?" At only seventy-one minutes, it's remarkably compact. The Criterion DVD includes an interesting conversation about the movie with filmmaker

> "You're convinced that the thing on this table isn't human. Do you know what it is, what I began with? An animal."
>
> —DR. MOREAU, *ISLAND OF LOST SOULS*

John Landis (*An American Werewolf in London*) and special effects makeup artist Rick Baker.

4. Stranger on the Third Floor

1940, directed by Boris Ingster. With Peter Lorre, John McGuire, Margaret Tallichet, Elisha Cook Jr., Charles Waldron

According to Gifford: "Peter Lorre fresh from M.*"*

This has been described as one of the very first film noir, that breed of moody crime dramas spiked with cynicism and unsavory sexuality whose golden age began shortly after World War II. The plot, about an ambitious young crime reporter who witnesses a murder and later is accused of a similar deed, is pretty straightforward—it isn't difficult to predict that he'll use his skills to find the real murderer. The shadowy dread, and Peter Lorre's brief but intense appearance as the title character, are what make this movie hum. Recently released by Warner Archive Collection in an excellent transfer, this brisk programmer (barely sixty minutes long) makes every moment count.

5. I Walked with a Zombie

1943, directed by Jacques Tourneur. With James Ellison, Frances Dee, Tom Conway, Theresa Harris, Sir Lancelot

According to Gifford: "Big nod to Val Lewton. Weird and wonderful take on Jane Eyre."

In the '40s, producer Val Lewton realized that you could create chills and atmosphere on a low budget. You didn't need expensive monsters or other special effects—using the tools of shadow and suggestion, the imagination of the viewer could be triggered to fill in the blanks. Set on a sugar plantation somewhere in the Caribbean, Tourneur's moody take on the Charlotte Brontë story eschews shock effects in favor of slow-building dread. This movie's zombies, by the way, aren't flesh-eating; they're of the mindless automaton variety.

6. The Red House

1947, directed by Delmer Daves. With Edward G. Robinson, Lon McCallister, Judith Anderson, Rory Calhoun, Julie London

According to Gifford: "Robinson in an unfairly ignored classic."

A farmer (Robinson) warns others to stay away from the title structure, lest they fall victim to its curse. But the forbidden is so hard to resist. The dark menace of the woods where much of the action takes place lends a haunting quality to the story's twists and turns. Sadly, because this film is now in the public domain, crummy DVDs and muddy-looking, hacked-up versions abound. If you ever have the chance to see it projected from film in a theater, don't hesitate!

7. Sunset Blvd.

1950, directed by Billy Wilder. With William Holden, Gloria Swanson, Erich von Stroheim, Nancy Olson, Cecil B. DeMille

According to Gifford: "The most chilling denouement in film history."

Fleeing repo men, desperate young screenwriter Joe Gillis (Holden) has the misfortune to seek refuge at the mansion of faded movie queen Norma Desmond (Swanson), who famously laments, "I *am* big—it's the *pictures* that got small!" Packed with crackling dialogue and loads of in-jokes, courtesy the Hollywood setting, this all-time classic has influenced everyone from the writers of *Seinfeld,* who reference it in several episodes, to David Lynch (see *Lost Highway* below). It's also the first movie to be narrated by a corpse!

8. Invaders from Mars

1953, directed by William Cameron Menzies. With Jimmy Hunt, Helena Carter, Arthur Franz, Morris Ankrum, Leif Erickson, Hillary Brooke

According to Gifford: "Check the backs of your parents' necks."

A little boy finds out that Martian invaders are slowly taking over the residents of his town, but of course none of the adults will believe him. Director Menzies was also a set designer and a pioneer in the use of color cinematography (he worked as special consultant on *Gone with the Wind*), and his talents are on full display in this sci-fi flick's eerie mood. The 1986 remake by Tobe Hooper has its own campy pleasures, but the original's wholesomely ironic 1950s-ness is tough to beat.

9. Cult of the Cobra

1955, directed by Francis D. Lyon. With Faith Domergue, Richard Long, Jack Kelly, Marshall Thompson, Myrna Hansen

According to Gifford: "Domergue was Howard Hughes's mistress."

With a title like that, what more can I add? A group of soldiers touring an Asian bazaar stumble upon a cult of women who can transform themselves into cobras at will. Naturally this discovery comes back to bite them (he-he). What it lacks in thrills or suspense, it makes up for in atmosphere (courtesy master cinematographer Russell Metty) and unintentional hilarity. With her dark, droopy eyes and battery of grimaces, Domergue is a perfect villainess.

10. The Night of the Hunter

1955, directed by Charles Laughton. With Robert Mitchum, Shelley Winters, Lillian Gish

According to Gifford: "Big nod to Davis Grubb. A noir poem."

Mitchum plays an unforgettable psychopath of the religious fanatical type. The Rev. Harry Powell has the words *LOVE* and *HATE* tattooed on his hands, and those very hands mete out their own brand of perverted justice in an all-consuming quest to recover a large sum of money taken in a robbery. Laughton's only film as director, based on a novel by Davis Grubb (love that name), uses the techniques of German Expressionism to fashion a sort of bleak rural film noir. Gish turns in a matchless performance as a shotgun-toting farm woman. The LOVE/HATE tattoos have been reused in many other films, most notably in *The Silence of the Lambs*.

11. Invasion of the Body Snatchers

1956, directed by Don Siegel. With Kevin McCarthy, Dana Wynter, King Donovan, Carolyn Jones, Larry Gates

According to Gifford: "Big nod to Jack Finney."

It's hard to overestimate the influence of this, one of the quintessential movies of the 1950s. Jack Finney's novel first appeared in serialized form in *Collier's* magazine. Although Finney always claimed that he had no political subtext in mind, the

In *The Night of the Hunter*, Robert Mitchum creates one of the screen's most memorable psychotics.

movie adaptation's pod people are the perfect metaphor for American conformity and/or Communists and/or anti-Communist hysteria.

12. Cape Fear

1962, directed by J. Lee Thompson. With Robert Mitchum, Gregory Peck, Polly Bergen, Telly Savalas

According to Gifford: "The original!"

No one played a sleepy-eyed pyscho better than Mitchum, and here he's aces as Max Cady, an ex-con rapist who holds lawyer Sam Bowden (Peck) personally responsible for his time in prison. He takes up residence near Bowden and begins a campaign of intimidation, getting a special kick out of targeting his wife and his 14-year-old daughter. Cady is a tinderbox of coiled violence ready to explode at any moment, and finally does in the suspenseful climax set on the family's houseboat. Razor-sharp black-and-white cinematography and a chilling score by Bernard Herrmann (Hitchcock's favorite composer) help make this a well-oiled thrill ride. Avoid Martin Scorsese's remake, starring Robert De Niro as Cady—it's a dopey, ham-fisted waste of time.

13. Repulsion

1965, directed by Roman Polanski. With Catherine Deneuve, Yvonne Furneaux, Ian Hendry, John Fraser, Patrick Wymark

According to Gifford: "Deneuve at her loveliest and most demented."

A beautiful (and mentally unstable) girl is left alone after her roommate goes out of town for the weekend. Shut up inside her apartment, gradually becoming disconnected from the outside world, she begins to experience disturbing hallucinations. Polanski contrasts the carefree, vibrant London of the Swinging Sixties outside with the skin-crawling claustrophobia of the girl's queasy isolation. The result is a slow-burning tale of insanity that will have you scrutinizing the cracks in your bedroom wall for days to come.

14. Série Noire

1979, directed by Alain Corneau. With Patrick Dewaere, Myriam Boyer, Marie Trintignant, Bernard Blier, Jeanne Herviale

According to Gifford: "From Jim Thompson's novel A Hell of a Woman *(1956), with a great performance by Dewaere."*

A rather dishonest door-to-door salesman, plying his trade in the shabby suburbs of Paris, encounters a teenaged femme fatale, who convinces him to murder her aunt. Also known under the banal title of *Thriller Story,* you won't find any of the "typical" French elegance on display here. No: it's as dark and brutal a thriller as anything as America has ever produced, loaded with bleakly comic touches that faithfully echo Thompson's original novel.

15. Lost Highway

1997, directed by David Lynch. With Patricia Arquette, Bill Pullman, Balthazar Getty, Robert Loggia, Robert Blake, Natasha Gregson Wagner

According to Gifford: "Big nod to myself."

David Lynch loves to play in the dark. In his world, there's sort-of dark, really dark, and pitch-black dark. They're put to gripping use in this twisted mutation of film noir. The most breathtaking example occurs in a shadowy hallway of the house of avant-garde sax player and demi-protagonist Fred Madison, who may or may not have murdered his wife. As he slowly walks down the hallway he moves from lightness to dark, appearing to gradually dissolve before our very eyes. The screenplay, by Barry Gifford and Lynch, like Lynch's more celebrated follow-up *Mulholland Dr.*, explores themes of doubling and identity. It's packed with haunting moments: an astonishingly disquieting sex scene, the eerie Natalie Woodishness of a leather-clad Natasha Gregson Wagner, a gorgeous use of This Mortal Coil's "Song to the Siren," Richard Pryor's out-of-left-field cameo (it was his final film), and Robert Blake's unforgettable performance as the enigmatic Mystery Man.

Robert Blake devised his own makeup for *Lost Highway*. His scene involving a cell phone call, which would be unthinkable to describe here, is unforgettable.

24

Ten Movies So Bad They're Good

For the most part this book has highlighted movies worth watching because of their superb craft and artistry. But it's only fitting to conclude with some movies at the other end of the spectrum. A genuinely terrible movie achieves a perfect disconnect between what the filmmakers intended and what actually ended up on-screen. A bad movie is honest; rather than the perfect illusion that a masterpiece creates, we instead see the warts-and-all of failure. And the results can be funnier than any comedy.

1. Reefer Madness

1938, directed by Louis J. Gasnier. With Dorothy Short, Kenneth Craig, Lillian Miles, Dave O'Brien, Thelma White, Warren McCollum, Carleton Young

Officially titled *Tell Your Children*, *Reefer Madness* is the granddaddy of all bad movies. This gritty exposé shows how a wholesome group of teenagers are driven to reckless driving, attempted rape, manslaughter, and an unsavory taste for jazz after just a few puffs of marijuana, "a violent narcotic, an unspeakable scourge, the real Public Enemy Number One." On video, check out the creatively colorized edition (with reefer smoke that changes color depending on the character) or the

RiffTrax version, featuring uproarious audio commentary by *Mystery Science Theater 3000* creators Mike Nelson, Bill Corbett, and Kevin Murphy.

2. Plan 9 from Outer Space

1959, directed by Edward D. Wood Jr. With Bela Lugosi, Gregory Walcott, Mona McKinnon, Tom Keene, Tor Johnson, Joanna Lee, John Breckinridge, Vampira

Their first eight plans to take over the world failed, but watch out! This group of sinister aliens has a ninth plan that's sure to succeed. Another oldie-but-baddie, this infamous cheapie from Ed Wood proves that a flaming paper plate does not make for a convincing spaceship. Incidentally, top-billed Lugosi actually appears in only a few scenes; he died before shooting was completed and was replaced by a tall man holding a cape over his face.

3. Earthquake

1974, directed by Mark Robson. With Charlton Heston, Ava Gardner, George Kennedy, Lorne Greene, Geneviève Bujold, Richard Roundtree, Marjoe Gortner, Barry Sullivan, Victoria Principal

Losing patience with his secretary, construction boss Sam Royce (Greene) barks, "Barbara! Take off your pantyhose, dammit!" It's my favorite line in this classic bad movie. The Big One finally hits LA, leading to mass destruction and mass unintentional hilarity. Gardner, only seven years younger than Greene, plays his *daughter*; Heston's frequent grimaces reveal an unfortunate lack of tartar control; and an *underground* shopping center is used as a postquake triage center. Then there's Gortner's creepy turn as a fro-haired sex maniac, and Walter Matthau's (wisely) unbilled cameo as a flamboyantly attired drunk. It's a bit depressing that this was one of 1974's biggest hits; then again, as the next movie's box office success demonstrates, the public's taste hadn't improved two years later . . .

4. Logan's Run

1976, directed by Michael Anderson. With Michael York, Richard Jordan, Jenny Agutter, Roscoe Lee Browne, Peter Ustinov

In the future, the remnants of mankind have retreated to a pleasure-filled existence inside some kind of a huge shopping mall, and everyone is killed off at the age of 30. York decides middle age might not be so bad after all and sets off to find out what's outside the utopian compound. A bastardization of the source novel by William F. Nolan and George Clayton Johnson, this dumbed-down groaner rips off better movies like *Planet of the Apes, THX-1138,* and Woody Allen's *Sleeper.* On the other hand it's a fascinating time capsule, telling us a lot more about 1976 than the

The original title of this Ed Wood classic, *Grave Robbers from Outer Space*, was changed after one of the movie's financial backers, a Baptist minister, objected.

future. Along with plenty of groovy Moog work on the soundtrack, we're treated to cheesy special effects (the sets look like some kind of elaborate hamster city) and incredibly dated costumes and hairstyles (mostly notably from Farrah Fawcett, in a small role as a bimbo receptionist).

5. The Apple

1980, directed by Menahem Golan. With Catherine Mary Stewart, George Gilmour, Vladek Sheybal, Grace Kennedy, Alan Love, Joss Ackland

Set in the futuristic year of 1994, which for some reason resembles a shopping mall in West Germany, this sterling morality tale concerns up-and-coming Canadian songwriters Alphie and Bibi, who win a music contest and are tempted into furthering their success by signing a contract with devilish music executive Mr. Boogalow. Oh yes—it's a musical. When the movie was first released, free copies of the soundtrack were given out, a practice that was hastily discontinued when audience members began to toss their record albums at the movie screen Frisbee-style. The songs are packed with witless rhymes and enhanced by terrible dance numbers. The ending, which I won't spoil for you, might almost be offensive if it weren't so laughable.

The best performances in *Showgirls* are those of Elizabeth Berkley's lips, by turns pouty and snarly.

6. Valley of the Dolls

1967, directed by Mark Robson. With Barbara Parkins, Patty Duke, Sharon Tate, Susan Hayward, Lee Grant, Tony Scotti, Martin Milner, Charles Drake, Joey Bishop

This staple of Best Worst Movies lists seemingly embraces every show-biz cliché in the book as it chronicles the ups and downs of three young women trying to make it on Broadway. It's also arguably the campiest homophobic movie ever made, with characters frequently spouting gay slurs even while mouthing some of the most ludicrous dialogue this side of a canceled soap opera: "They drummed you right outta Hollywood! So ya come crawlin' back to Broadway. Well, Broadway doesn't go for booze and dope. Now you get outta my way, I got a guy waitin' for me." Meanwhile, Dionne Warwick sings the movie's theme song about fifty times too many. Look fast for Richard Dreyfuss in a split-second role as an assistant stage manager. Roger Ebert (!) penned the screenplay for the belated follow-up, *Beyond the Valley of the Dolls.*

7. Showgirls

1995, directed by Paul Verhoeven. With Elizabeth Berkley, Kyle MacLachlan, Gina Gershon, Glenn Plummer, Robert Davi, Alan Rachins, Gina Ravera

Berkley pounds a bottle of ketchup into submission and later has porpoise-like intercourse in MacLachlan's swimming pool in this howlingly trashy story about an airheaded dancer who will stop at nothing to be the top showgirl in Vegas. Verhoeven and screenwriter Joe Eszterhas take *All about Eve,* add a dollop of *Valley of the Dolls,* and tart it up with crass materialism and some of the most unerotic sex scenes ever captured. A flop at the box office, it has since become a cult classic on video.

8. The Room

2003, directed by Tommy Wiseau. With Tommy Wiseau, Juliette Danielle, Greg Sestero, Philip Haldiman, Kyle Vogt, Carolyn Minnott, Robyn Paris

> "You betrayed me! You're not good. You, you're just a chicken. Cheep-cheep-cheep-cheep-cheep-cheep."
>
> –JOHNNY, *THE ROOM*

Picture *Showgirls* as a chamber piece, looking like it cost about $14.99 to produce. That's a close approximation of *The Room.* A lumpy clone of Fabio, sporting a peculiar accent that sounds like Marseilles by way of the Bronx, Wiseau wrote, directed, produced, and stars (as Johnny) in this atrocity, a ridiculously hysterical melodrama about infidelity among a group of friends in San Francisco. Its queasy combination of awkward sex scenes, wooden acting, terrible dialog, and illogical continuity must be seen to be disbelieved. *The Room* is now a *Rocky Horror Picture Show*–style sensation, with midnight audiences in several cities enthusiastically playing along with the on-screen action, often with Wiseau himself attending!

9. Body of Evidence

1993, directed by Uli Edel. With Madonna, Willem Dafoe, Joe Mantegna, Anne Archer, Frank Langella, Julianne Moore, Jürgen Prochnow

It seems almost cruel (and unnecessary) to call attention to Madonna's remarkable lack of ability as an actress, which is on full display here. But it's only one terrible element in a silly "thriller" that's loaded with them. The former Material Girl plays an enigmatic temptress suspected by the district attorney (Mantegna) of killing her rich old husband. The method? An overdose of rough sex. Meanwhile, she puts the moves on her defense lawyer (Dafoe) with the help of bondage and candle wax. The otherwise talented cast (look at that roster!) undoubtedly held their noses with one hand while endorsing their paychecks with the other.

10. Troll 2

1990, directed by Claudio Fragasso. With Michael Stephenson, George Hardy, Margo Prey, Connie Young, Deborah Reed, Jason F. Wright, Darren Ewing, Jason Steadman

Despite the title, it's not connected to the 1986 movie *Troll* and does not actually feature trolls. Instead it's one of the very few examples of a vegetarian horror movie, the gripping tale of a dastardly plot by evil goblins to turn human beings into plants. The screenplay was written by Italians with a shaky grasp of English, and brought to life by a group of actors whose skill can charitably be described as "enthusiastic." A cult movie of the highest order, it's even inspired a documentary chronicling the phenomenon, *Best Worst Movie*.

Movie Resources

This list is not meant to be comprehensive in any way; these are just some of the resources that I myself find the most useful. They're terrific for reference purposes as well as learning about movies and generating movie viewing suggestions.

WEBSITES

AV Club

www.avclub.com

AV Club is pop culture commentary with an attitude. But it's also consistently well informed and exceedingly articulate. Refreshingly, these are writers whose memories of cinema stretch back to the silent era; they're just as apt to turn you on to a black-and-white classic as to praise the latest Wes Anderson movie. Pieces cover current theatrical releases, new DVDs, and blasts from the past.

David Bordwell's Website on Cinema

www.davidbordwell.net

David Bordwell is easily one of the most astute observers of cinematic trends, and his writings distill and clarify the often confusing mechanics of how movies are made and perceived. His website includes a blog and great links to other cinema resources, as well as an ongoing series of thoughtful essays. A recent one, written with Kristin Thompson, examines the ramifications of all-digital filmmaking and distribution—it's a must-read.

DVD Verdict

www.dvdverdict.com

DVD Verdict features witty judgments on new DVDs. Its reviewers are especially adept at comparing new Blu-ray discs to previous DVD incarnations, evaluating whether or not the "upgrade" is actually worth the purchase. The site also offers podcasts and sections with interviews and movie news.

Ferdy on Films

www.ferdyonfilms.com

Loaded with film reviews of recent releases as well as longer essays reflecting on movie history, Ferdy on Films, from Marilyn Ferdinand and Roderick Heath, presents uncommonly articulate perspectives on a wide range of cinema. There have been numerous times when I've changed my mind about a movie after reading what Ferdy on Films had to say about it.

Filmspotting

filmspotting.net

Filmspotting offers reviews, interviews, lists, and a weekly podcast from film fans who really know their stuff. iPhone/Android apps make access easy.

Goatdog's Movies

goatdog.com

Cheekily billed "The greatest movie review site in the history of ever," Goatdog's Movies rates films on a scale of 0 to 4 goats, encompassing current releases, DVDs, and whatever else cinemaniac Mike Phillips feels like. His "stinker of the month" list is the perfect way to find your next bad movie.

GreenCine

www.greencine.com

If you live on the West Coast and aren't that interested in streaming movies, GreenCine, a DVD-by-mail subscription service, is definitely worth checking out. Geared toward independent, documentary, and foreign films in addition to DVD rentals, GreenCine also boasts coverage of the filmmaking scene, with reports from film festivals and interviews with filmmakers.

IMDb

www.imdb.com

The Internet Movie Database is a free online resource that aims to collect information about every movie ever made. Invaluable for tracking down filmographies and release information. But beware: like Wikipedia, it's not error-free.

Mubi

mubi.com

Mubi is a marvelous movie portal offering an ongoing cornucopia of movie news and thoughtful essays. You can also stream many movies from Mubi, some for free. Lively forums offer the chance to connect with other movie lovers all over the world, and the Mubi Garage is a sort of online movie school where filmmakers can test out ideas and share their work.

Roger Ebert's Website

rogerebert.com

It should go without saying that Roger Ebert's website really has no equal when it comes to movies. Whether or not you agree with his views, his perspective will help you avoid the mindless consumption of empty movie calories. His articulation of why 3-D is such a terrible idea has galvanized many filmgoers (including me). Besides reviews, there are sections with news, interviews, in-depth commentary, and Ebert's wonderful blog.

They Shoot Pictures, Don't They?

theyshootpictures.com

They Shoot Pictures, Don't They? is a fantastic site combining "best of" lists from hundreds of critics, filmmakers, and celebrities into giant, searchable indexes that cover the most acclaimed movies ever made. If you're looking for more ideas on what to watch next, this site is the place to go.

BOOKS

The Age of Movies: Selected Writings of Pauline Kael

Edited by Sanford Schwartz (New York: Library of America, 2011).

Reading film reviews by Pauline Kael can be frustrating. She seemed to be tone-deaf to certain kinds of filmmaking. Yet to read her reviews championing the likes of Robert Altman and Francis Ford Coppola is to feel truly exhilarated. Like the best critics (and she was film critic for the *New Yorker* from 1968 to 1991), she gets you going, and this recent collection is great one to dip into when the mood strikes you.

Cult Movies: The Classics, the Sleepers, the Weird, and the Wonderful
By Danny Peary (New York: Gramercy, 1998)
Peary rounds up a variety of films that have inspired fevered devotion, providing plot summaries and commenting on their appeal. Practically every film he includes is worth watching (if only to find out what all the fuss is about).

Goodbye Cinema, Hello Cinephilia: Film Culture in Transition
Jonathan Rosenbaum (Chicago: University of Chicago, 2010)
It's a bad time to be a movie lover but a great time to be a cinephile, argues Rosenbaum in this invigorating collection. Pieces like "In Defense of Spoilers" and "Bushwacked Cinema" help us to see old films with fresh eyes, and other essays inspire us to seek out the undeservedly obscure.

Leonard Maltin's Classic Movie Guide: From the Silent Era through 1965
By Leonard Maltin (London: Penguin, 2011)
A companion volume to his main movie guide (see next entry), this book takes an in-depth look at movies released before 1966. He profiles a lot of series films, like Westerns and the Andy Hardy series.

Leonard Maltin's 2013 Movie Guide: The Modern Era
Edited by Leonard Maltin (New York: Signet, 2012)
If I could have only one film reference book, this would be it. Capsules, running times, cast lists, and reviews of about thirteen thousand movies make it a paradise for browsing. Of course, you have to learn to read the reviews with a grain of salt—the dismissals of certain movies (*Blue Velvet*) and the inexplicable raves for others (four stars for *The Cider House Rules*?!) can be maddening. Nevertheless, in terms of sheer scope Maltin's guide has no equal. Updated annually.

Movie Wars: How Hollywood and the Media Conspire to Limit What Movies We Can See
By Jonathan Rosenbaum (Chicago: Cappella, 2000)
If you've ever wondered why the movies showing at your multiplex just seem to get worse and worse every year (and who hasn't?), reading Rosenbaum's book will lead to many aha moments. He lays out a very convincing argument that it's in the

best interests of the media industry to homogenize our movie choices—releasing sequels and other movies derived from existing "brands" simply ensures a greater return on investment for the studios then having to nurture original ideas.

The New Biographical Dictionary of Film, 5th Ed.
By David Thomson (New York: Knopf, 2010)
Hundreds of biographical sketches make up this entertaining volume. Awesomely opinionated, Thomson can be snide ("I remain uncertain about everything except the absence of a flawless film in Altman's work") and snobbish ("[Cary Grant] was the best and most important actor in the history of cinema.") Yet he can also be very perceptive. In any case, the forcefulness of his convictions will make you question your own, and they offer much food for thought.

Reel Conversations: Candid Interviews with Film's Foremost Directors and Critics
By George Hickenlooper (New York: Carol Publishing Group, 1991).
George A. Romero, David Lynch, John Carpenter, David Cronenberg, Paul Verhoeven, and Dennis Hopper are among those whom Hickenlooper talks with in this impressive collection.

ARTICLES

"The Greatest Films of All Time 2012"
Sight & Sound 22.9 (September 2012). Also at www.bfi.org.uk/polls-surveys/greatest-films-all-time-2012.
Famously described by Roger Ebert as "by far the most respected of the countless polls of great movies—the only one most serious movie people take seriously," the *Sight & Sound* movie poll has been conducted by the magazine every ten years since 1952. The newest poll, featuring some relatively recent movies, definitely has some surprises. If you want to check out what hundreds of the most influential and respected filmmakers and critics consider the greatest movies of all time, look no further.

"Post Focus: Paramount Restores *The Godfather*"
By Stephanie Argy (*American Cinematographer*, May 2008)
Argy details the extraordinary work of restoring the legendary movie, which was in sorry shape after decades of abuse.

DVDS

Treasures of American Film Archives: 50 Preserved Films
(National Film Preservation Foundation and Image Entertainment, 2000)
This four-disc set is worthy of special attention. Among the nearly eleven hours of priceless films: an adaptation of *Snow White* from 1916, scenes from Orson Welles's 1936 "Voodoo" *Macbeth*, 1933 home movies from Groucho Marx, and a 1943 Private Snafu cartoon written by Dr. Seuss and directed by Chuck Jones.

Wholphin
www.wholphindvd.com
I'm afraid that I've given short films the short end of the stick in this book. But a good short can act as the perfect lead-in to the "feature presentation" during your movie night. This DVD magazine created by Dave Eggers and Brent Hoff of McSweeney's is published quarterly and spotlights some of the funniest, most clever (and sometimes most affecting) shorts produced, from all over the world. And as with any magazine, there's no need to devour the whole thing in one sitting—you can sample the pieces one at time.

Index

Recommended movies are in **bold**.